The Deluxe Unofficial Guide to Battle Royale

The
BIG BOOK OF
FORTNITE

This book is available in quantity at special discounts for your group or organization. For further information, contact:

Triumph Books LLC
814 North Franklin Street
Chicago, Illinois 60610
Phone: (312) 337-0747
www.triumphbooks.com

Printed in U.S.A.
978-1-62937-640-0

Content packaged by Mojo Media, Inc.
Joe Funk: Editor
Jason Hinman: Creative Director
Samantha M Skinner: Writer

CONTENTS

Introduction

FORTNITE IS THE POPULAR BATTLE ROYALE STYLE GAME THAT'S TAKEN THE WORLD BY STORM. Whether you are a gamer or not, chances are very good that you've at least heard of the game at this point, and you've probably even seen someone playing it if you haven't tried it yourself. The game focuses on putting groups of 100 players against one another in a fight for survival. Groups can be made up of four per team, two per team or 100 indiviual players all vying for the top spot in the game. No matter what format players decide to play in, one thing stays the same, they will be running around, finding as much valuable loot as they can, and fighting for their survival while trying to become the last remaining player in the game.

Fortnite is an intense death-match styled game, but it's more than that. It's a test of skill and it's a colorful and fun experience. Many new players are overwhelmed by the controls, all the different places on the map and all the enemies trying to take them out, but over time as the game becomes more familiar it has a sort of charm to it. Fortnite is a long-term game of skill that takes time to get good at, and it's a game that players of all ages can enjoy. It's available on most game systems today, including PlayStation 4, Xbox One, PC, Nintendo Switch, iOS and Android, and it can be played by just about anyone.

Why Play Fortnite?

Even if you've tried Fortnite out before, or you've seen someone else play the game, you might be wondering why you should play the game personally. That's a hard question to answer, but the game has a lot going for it. While it seems like a basic shooter and survival game on the surface, it's actually much more than that. Fortnite adds in an element of building that makes things much more interesting and challenging. The best players put up complex structures while battling their enemies, and it's through their building skills that they often determine who is going to win or lose a match. If you enjoy shooting games you'll probably like some of the features that Fortnite has to offer, but even if you get bored with standard shooters you may still enjoy this game.

Fortnite demands a high level of skill from the gamers that want to be good at it. You will spend time learning to build properly. You will spend time learning different areas of the map and how to best use their features to meet your own needs. Only after taking the time to learn all these different things will you stand a chance at beating the other players that you come up against. The game gives you a chance to develop your skills and learn to use your creativity to overcome enemies. It's bright and colorful and a lot of fun for kids and adults alike, and thanks to all the different challenges, special customization items and the leveling system, you'll always have a goal to work toward as you play round after round of this challenging game on whatever system you decide to use.

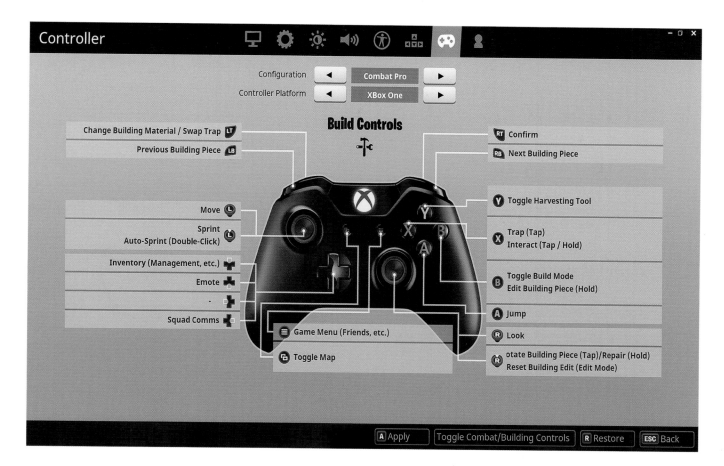

GETTING YOUR CONTROLS DOWN

There are few games on the market today that can match the complexity of Fortnite while still making an easy game to pick up and start playing. It's simple enough to get going with, but over time you'll realize there is much more under the surface. Gamers that enjoy a challenge will love this game. Gamers that like collecting items will get a kick out of playing regularly, and the game is completely free if you don't purchase any of the extra premium content available for it.

What You'll Learn with this Guide

Now that you know you want to play Fortnite, it's time to figure out how to play it as effectively as possible. In this guide we'll cover every aspect of the game from in-depth building strategies to help you climb up above your enemies and trap them in a box, to a major weapon guide helping you figure out exactly which guns you should be picking up as you go from one spot on the map to the next.

GETTING YOUR CONTROLS DOWN

Throughout this guide we will explain about the different controls you need to use to manipulate the game. We won't just give you an overview of the controls, because you can see that in the game itself. Instead, we'll walk you through the concepts behind the controls, so you get how to use them effectively and what all those different control buttons really mean. Just looking at the controls for the game will seem daunting at first, but with our breakdown you'll be much more comfortable playing the game.

LEARNING ABOUT THE ITEMS

There are dozens of items in Fortnite, and you need to understand the purpose of each one. In this in-depth guide we overview each of the different items and what they are good for. You'll learn about all the different weapon types and rarities, the different traps, the grenades, the materials and consumables, and you'll learn how to make use of every single one of them properly.

① LEARN TO BUILD

Building is the most important and more difficult of all the Fortnite skills. Learn how to make basic structures, advanced structures and how to edit the items that you lay down. We'll also teach you tips and tricks to build more effectively no matter what system you play the game on.

② LEVELING UP

Gaining levels will give you a sense of accomplishment and help you earn Battle Stars for premium items. We explain how to level up effectively and make the most of all your time in Fortnite. Stop wasting your play time and make the most of each match that you enter.

③ CHOOSING A STARTING LOCATION

Deciding where in that massive world to drop down to at the start of a match in Fortnite is daunting, but we're here to help. We'll explain more about some of the best starting locations in the game and how you can make the most of each one. Don't get overwhelmed by all the different options. Read through our quick guide and pick a location that fits your play personality. You'll find some locations to be better than others, so test out a few and decide on the one you like the best.

MAKING USE OF THE BATTLE PASS

The Battle Pass is an excellent purchase to enhance your Fortnite experience, but it's one that you shouldn't make lightly. We'll help you decide if you want the pass or not, and teach you how to make the most of your pass as well. We'll explain how to tier up effectively and about what sort of benefits you can expect from the pass once you have it. We even explain how to get your next Battle Pass for free!

GETTING PREMIUM ITEMS

There's an overwhelming amount of content for Fortnite, much of which you have to pay for. With so many different skins, contrails, emotes, gliders and more to choose from, you'll quickly be overwhelmed and start wondering which options make sense. We'll walk you through the different options, help you figure out how to get some of those customization items for free, and explain what you should do to get the right items for your character specifically.

LEARNING FROM AND BECOMING A FORTNITE PRO

Today there are dozens of professional Fortnite players like Ninja or Myth and more are turning up all the time. These elite players are known for their high level of skill, but also for having followers online. With so many professional players available to watch online it's easy to learn high level skills and to enhance your game by watching their matches. Learn about the top Fortnite players and what you can take from them to improve your own game. Also learn what it takes to become a professional Fortnite player yourself.

USING THIS GUIDE TO ITS FULL POTENTIAL

Fortnite is a blast to play when done right, and it's something that you can do with friends, family members and anyone you know that likes to game. With that said, it can be overwhelming and a bit disheartening too. It's upsetting getting killed in the first 30 seconds of a match over and over again, and that's why we're here to help. Make use of this guide to help improve your game.

Use our guide to teach you where you should drop out of the bus. Use the guide to learn which weapon loadout makes the most sense for you and how you can optimize your character properly.

We explain step-by-step how you can become more effective at Fortnite and get the best play experience possible out of it. It's not going to be easy to become a top-level player, but with our help it will be much more likely. Just make sure that you are reading through the most important sections of our guide to learn the skills that you need to know to do well, and you'll start having success in the game.

We're not promising you that this guide will make you an expert Fortnite player that gets more than a dozen kills per match. We are promising you that it will teach you more about the game, help you figure out what you need to improve, and make sure that you are getting better with each match that you play. Read through our advice and use it to figure out what to do to get better at the game. You'll start to feel better about Fortnite over time with our guide, and you might end up being one of the best Fortnite players out of everyone you know as well!

To make the most of this guide read through the Getting Started in Fortnite section, and read through the Understanding the Basics section, but then feel free to skip around to the sections that are most interesting to you. You'll learn something different about the game in each one of them and should be able to get more out of your time with the game after reading them. ★

Getting Started

FORTNITE IS ONE OF THE MOST POPULAR GAMES IN THE WORLD RIGHT NOW, and it's easy to see why you would want to give it a try. For many people getting started is as simple as downloading the game, creating an account and giving the game a try, but for others it might mean buying a new computer or game console first. If you're interested in getting started with the game, we'll take the time to break down each of the steps you'll need to follow. Don't worry, it's not difficult to start playing Fortnite, and with our help you could be testing out the game today!

Choosing Your Platform for Fortnite

When it comes to running Fortnite well, there are a few different system options you have to work with. You can play on a PlayStation 4, an Xbox One, a PC or MAC computer or a newer Apple phone or tablet. Each option offers real benefits, but players should pick from options they already have, or choose a system that makes the most sense for them.

Playing on a Console

For console players you can pick up the game and run it smoothly on either an Xbox One or a PlayStation 4. The game will run perfectly fine on the standard Xbox One, but the Xbox One X will do a good job as well. PlayStation gamers can enjoy smooth gameplay on a standard PS4, or they can go with the upgraded PlayStation 4 Pro with good results.

Playing on Computer

For computer players whether on a PC or Mac system, it's important that you have a modern device that meets all the necessary system requirements. Your system should ideally meet the recommended requirements outlined below, but if you have a computer that meets the minimum requirements you should have no trouble running the game, though you'll have to keep the graphics settings lower as you play.

THE MINIMUM REQUIREMENTS

✔ Graphics Card – Intel HD 4000
✔ CPU – Core i3 2.4 Ghz
✔ RAM – 4 GB

RECOMMENDED REQUIREMENTS

✔ Graphics Card – AMD Radeon 7870 or Nvidia GTX 660
✔ CPU – Core i5 2.8 Ghz
✔ RAM – 8 GB

Playing on Mobile

While playing Fortnite on a tablet or phone will take some getting used to, it can be a fun way to enjoy the popular game while away from home. In order to enjoy this fast-paced shooter on mobile you need to have a modern iOS device like the iPhone SE, 6S, 7, 8 or X if you want to play on phone. If you would rather game on a tablet you can use an iPad Mini 4 or an iPad Air 2 as long as it's the 2017 or Pro versions. The mobile device you use needs to have iOS 11 or newer and older devices like the iPhone 6, 6 Plus and older simply won't work.

Signing up and Creating an Account

Now that you have the system you want to play on, you'll need an active Epic Games account to use for Fortnite. To create an account simply visit www.epicgames.com/Fortnite and select the "Get Fortnite" button. Once you do that you'll be taken to the following form where you can easily make your new account.

When creating an account for console you can speed up the creation process by using your PlayStation or Xbox account information as your account sign-on. To do this click on the Xbox or PlayStation account buttons above the form. You can also use your Google or Facebook account to quickly create an Epic Games account. If you don't want to use an existing account, skip the buttons up top and fill out all the form fields below. Check that you've read and agree to the terms of service and then click "Create Account" and you'll have your new Epic Games account to play on.

With your new account created you can now download the game to your PC, mobile device, or console and start playing. Just make sure you write down your account information so you can link your account when you're ready to play.

Choosing a Game Mode

The moment that you load up Fortnite: Battle Royale, you'll have to choose from one of the available game modes. There are a few standard modes that are always present, and unique limited time game modes like the famous 50 versus 50 deathmatch. We're just covering the standard modes in this guide to keep things simple and friendly to new players.

SOLO

It's you against the world in Solo mode. You'll be all out there on your own trying to survive against 99 other players all with the same goal in mind. It's up to you to outsmart them, outshoot them and claw your way to the top of the heap in this ultimate survival challenge! Solo is perfect for those times when nobody on your friends list is on, or when you feel like going it alone and not sticking around with any other players.

DUOS

Group up with one of your friends and go head to head against 49 other teams of 2 to try to take first place. This is the perfect game mode for a gamer with a single friend ready to play. Stick close to your partner because they're all you have to rely on!

SQUADS

Group up in teams of 4 and try to be the last remaining team out of the 25 involved in the action. In this mode teamwork and communication are key, and it's vital that you stick together with the other players in your group. If you have three other friends you want to play with, this is the perfect option for you!

TO FILL OR NOT TO FILL

With Duos and Squads you'll have an option that says Fill or Don't Fill. This is an important selection that needs some consideration. If you have the maximum number of players in your group for the chosen game mode you won't have to worry about the option, but when you're queued for Duos on your own, or Squads with less than four, you have to decide if you want to keep your small group or if you want to fill it with strangers. You can go up against other pairs on your own, or other squads with less than a full group of

4 by choosing "Don't Fill". If you don't mind grouping with strangers and you want a full group and the best chances for victory, choose "Fill".

TESTING OUT THE LIMITED GAME MODES

The creators of Fortnite release a range of limited game modes that are available for a short period of time. These modes include things like 50 versus 50, Sniper Shootout, the Infinity Gauntlet, High Explosives and more. In these special game types you'll have access to different weapons, different win conditions and a whole new game essentially. They're fun to play while they last, but eventually they'll be removed for something else. That's why it's best to practice in the normal game modes if you want to get better, because mastering a limited time game type won't help you win anymore once it's removed.

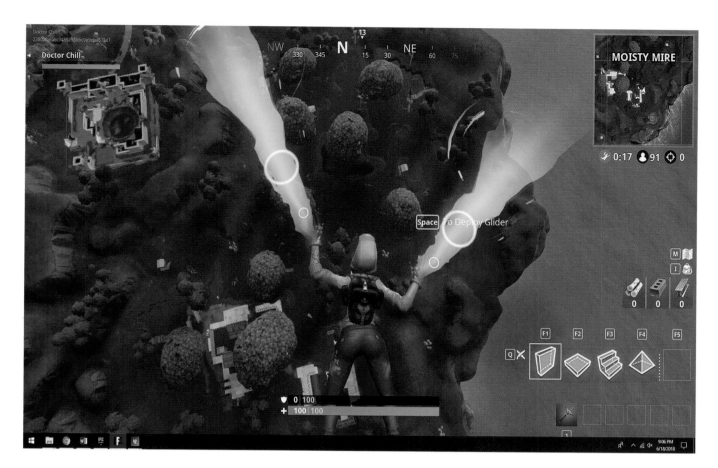

Playing Your First Round

So you have your account setup, you've loaded up the game and you've chosen a game type to try out. Now it's time to play through your first round of Fortnite! If you're anything like me you're probably feeling a mixture of excitement and nervousness while waiting for that loading screen, but don't worry, I'll walk you through your first round of the game.

From the moment you select Play the game will begin to load and you'll be taken to the lobby. In the lobby you can run around, pick up weapons to practice with or materials to craft with while you wait for all 100 players to show up for the match. Once they arrive you'll be taken to the Battle Bus to get ready to start the match.

CHOOSE A STARTING SPOT

Once aboard the bus you can load up the game's map and pick out your starting location. There's a special marker tool, letting you set a waypoint on the map. Set your starting location, or just jump out randomly and see how it goes.

The bus will fly from one side of the map to the other, and you are free to jump out at any point. It's best to avoid jumping at the beginning or the end of the path, because more players will get off at those two points than any other. Once you jump, aim your character down as steeply as possible so you'll fall as fast as you can to your final destination.

LOOTING AND GATHERING

Now that you're down on the ground it's time to get looting as fast as possible. Search surrounding houses, trucks, shipping containers, camps and more for prized loot that will help you survive. You want to grab a gun as soon as possible, and equip it to fight off any early attackers. Once you have your first gun you should begin looking for shield potions, more powerful weapons and additional tools like grenades or med packs to help you stay alive.

During this early looting phase you also need to be gathering materials, or you'll be in trouble when your enemies are building up ramps and walls and you're stuck out in the open. Equip your pickaxe and gather materials from houses, trees, cars, pallets or most other items throughout the world to build up a stockpile of wood, brick and metal.

MOVING AND FIGHTING

Once you've looted up some open up your map to see where the eye of the storm is. You must avoid the pink sections of the map and remain in the circle at all times. Follow the white line on your minimap to remain in the circle and keep moving each time the storm is closing in to avoid taking serious storm damage.

As you move around the world look around for other players. Try to spot them before they spot you, and stay out of the open as much as possible. Try and equip a shotgun or pistol for close quarters fighting whenever you are inside a building, and go with something like an SMG, assault rifle or sniper rifle when outside moving around. If you see an enemy, sneak up on them as close as you can and then open fire on them! Don't be discouraged if you get taken out, this is all part of the learning process and you'll get better over time.

TRYING TO WIN

In order to win your match you need to reach the center of the map and you need to take out any remaining players. Keep following the storm circle as you play and try to pick a high location or to hide within buildings whenever you can to help give you an edge over your opponents. It's highly unlikely that you'll win your first match ever in Fortnite, but it's not a bad idea. Survive as long as you can and do your best to get a kill and you'll be well on your way to success in this hit online shooter!

Adjusting Graphics Settings
(For PC and MAC Players)

Whether you're playing Fortnite on a high powered gaming machine, or you're using a PC that's just barely over the minimum system requirements, there are some optimizations that you can make to ensure that the game runs smoother. The smoother your gameplay, the easier it is to land headshots, to outbuild your opponents and to come out on top with a sweet victory. If you want a smoother gaming experience make the recommended changes to your in-game settings and you should notice a nice improvement.

GETTING TO THE SETTINGS

✔ Load up Fortnite: Battle Royale and select the "Settings" menu by selecting the three lines button at the top right of the screen.

✔ Change "Window Mode" to "Fullscreen" if it isn't already.

✔ Switch "Frame Rate" to "Unlimited".

✔ Set "3D Resolution" to "100%".

✔ Switch the "View Distance" to "Medium".

✔ Turn Shadows and Anti-Aliasing off.

✔ Change the "Textures" setting to "Medium".

✔ Change "Effects" to the "Low" setting level.

✔ Switch "Post Processing" to "Low".

✔ Shut off "Vsync" and "Motion Blur" and "Show Grass".

By making all of these simple changes you will help your game perform more smoothly and increase your chances of winning. ★

Understanding the Basics

THERE IS QUITE A BIT TO LEARN BEFORE YOU'LL BE HAVING SUCCESS IN FORTNITE. First, you'll have to come to grips with the different controls. From there you need to learn about starting locations and where you want to drop down when you're getting used to the game. Once you master those two things you'll want to move on to learning about weapons and what their rarities mean and how to best use the different types that you find on the ground. We'll also cover consumables and what you should be picking up and using throughout a match. Finally, we'll focus in on building effective structures to keep you alive, and leveling up and improving your character. All this takes time to learn, but it's worth the effort because it will make you more comfortable in Fortnite, and you'll be happy that you're beginning to improve in the game.

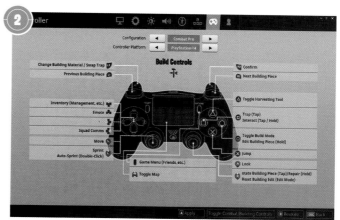

Learning the Controls

Getting the hang of the basic Fortnite controls is an important first step before you begin playing the game. Learn how to manipulate the world a bit and you'll be much more comfortable when you get into the game itself.

① PC

MOVING: Run around the screen using the WASD keys on your keyboard. Jump with the spacebar, and crouch using the Left Ctrl key.

Toggle sprint on and off by holding Shift down. And look around by moving the mouse around.

FIGHTING: Pick items up using E, and quickly toggle from one to the next using 2, 3, 4, 5 and 6 for the different inventory slots. You can also swap through inventory slots using the mouse scroll wheel.

Aim your weapon using the mouse, look down the sights with the right mouse click and fire with a left mouse click.

Reload your weapon with R.

MANAGING YOUR INVENTORY: Open the inventory with the I key. Move objects between slots by left mouse clicking, holding and dragging from one slot to another.

BASIC BUILDING: Select building pieces using the F1 through F4 keys on the keyboard and lay down the piece

with a left click on your mouse. Grab traps by pressing the F5 key and lay them down with a mouse left click.

Edit items using the G key and then toggle the edit squares on and off with left clicks from your mouse. Accept the edits with the G key.

② XBOX ONE

MOVING: Use the left analog stick to move your character around the screen. Press the stick down to make your character sprint around the map.

Use the A button to jump up and down and press down the right analog stick to crouch down and to stand back up again.

FIGHTING: Start battle with picking up weapons and consumables. Use the X button to pick up weapons and other items off the ground. You can easily switch between weapons by pressing down the RB and LB buttons to go between your five item slots.

The right analog stick is your tool for aiming. Use it to lock onto targets and then press RT to fire weapons when you have them equipped. Zoom in and aim more accurately at your enemies using LT before firing to get a better shot.

MANAGING YOUR INVENTORY: If you don't like the order that your items are in, you can open up your inventory by pressing the UP button on the D-pad of your controller. Once open you can easily swap items by pressing A on the item and pressing A on the slot you want to move it to.

BASIC BUILDING: To harvest items in Fortnite press Y to get your pickaxe out and press RT to strike material sources in front of you.

Press B to switch over to builder mode. When that's open you can swap between materials with RB and LB. Place items with RT and edit them by holding down B after they are already down.

Fortnite will automatically switch between materials when you run out of one, but you can manually switch materials with LT.

When you are finished building press B again to switch back to combat mode.

⊘ PLAYSTATION 4

MOVING: Use the left Analog stick to run around and press it down to make your character sprint. Jump with the X button and crouch by pressing L1. You can stand back up from a crouch by pressing L1 again as well.

FIGHTING: Pick items and consumables up out in the world with the Square button. Easily switch between your inventory slots using the Triangle button. Press it to move forward from one weapon to the next.

When you see an enemy use the right stick to aim at them and L2 to aim down the sights of your gun. Fire with R2 and reload with Square.

MANAGE YOUR INVENTORY: Use the PS4 track pad to open the inventory and to quickly move items through the different inventory slots using the analog stick and X.

BASIC BUILDING: Hold Triangle to get your pickaxe out and press R2 to swing and gather materials.

Swap from one building piece to the next by repeatedly tapping Triangle. Lay down the piece by pressing R2.

Rotate a building piece with R1 and select a trap by tapping Square. Hold Circle on a laid building piece to edit it and press Circle to confirm the change.

Choosing a Starting Location

Whether you are new to Fortnite or a seasoned pro, choosing a starting location is one of the most important decisions that you'll make early on in the game. It determines how much loot you have access to, how many materials you can gather and whether or not you're going to have to fight for your life early on. Choose too busy of a location and you'll have plenty of loot to pick up and make use of, but you'll be attacked within minutes of landing. Choose an area that's too deserted and you'll be safe to gather materials and start stockpiling weapons, but you won't have very much loot to gather. It's important to decide on a play style that you want to go with early on, and then pick a starting location that matches that play style. You can also choose a starting location based on the skills that you want to learn in the game.

Balanced Starting Locations

These starting locations balance threat level with loot to offer the best of both worlds. They aren't extremely dangerous to land at, and there is plenty of loot to get you started in a new round of the game. Choose one of these for a balanced approach to the match.

⊙ LOOT LAKE

Loot Lake is located right near the center of the map and almost always within the storm circle. This makes this location a leisurely spot to drop down and really search for loot, and there is plenty of it! Loot Lake has 12 different chest locations with some around the edges of the lake and others right in the center. Players can grab a great deal of loot by dropping on the side of the lake nearest to Anarchy Acres or the side nearest to Pleasant Park. Just make sure to take cover early on and to grab up whatever loot you can.

When crossing Loot Lake it's a good idea to build a platform to move as quickly as possible to make it more difficult for other players to pick you off as you move.

FLUSH FACTORY

Flush Factory is an excellent location for new players to drop at, but it must be used with care. When the bus flight pattern does not cross over Flush Factory initially, you can safely drop down here and pick up the many chests that are all located near each other. There is plenty of loot to go around at this location as long as you hit the proper spots.

The large truck out in the front courtyard often has a chest in the back. The shipping container to the west side of the yard often holds a chest as well. Once you grab those two, you can head around the side of the building, and go down the ramp to the hidden chest under the archway connected to the factory building itself. It will be behind a green container hiding it from plain view.

If those three chests aren't enough, or if you are the only person in Flush Factory, there are several additional chests within the factory itself for you to explore.

⑤ HAUNTED HILLS

Haunted Hills is a fun and well-balanced started location in Fortnite that actually offers excellent loot potential. This is a more dangerous starting location than Flush Factory, but is about on par with Loot Lake. When you drop at Haunted Hills there are chests in most of the buildings, so be sure to check them all! The largest building of the bunch almost always has a chest down in its basement, and often has one up above as well, so this is a good starting location to work from.

The only trouble with Haunted Hills is that it is so close to Pleasant Park and often gets a decent amount of foot traffic for this very reason. If you aren't comfortable with fighting just yet, you will gain some experience dropping in Haunted Hills for sure.

Defensive Starting Locations

For less experienced Fortnite players it's often best to start in more remote and defense-focused locations than it is to start in high action locations. You'll get in fewer fights, while still having a chance to grab some pretty decent loot and tons of materials in our two defensive starting locations, Wailing Woods and Moisty Mire.

◎ WAILING WOODS

Wailing Woods is one of the safest locations to start off in. There is plenty of cover to hide you from enemies and there are some pretty decent chests in the area as well. Not only that, but there are tons of huge trees for you to chop down to give you plenty of wood to build up and around your enemies with.

The trick to getting decent loot in Wailing Woods is to drop down right inside the maze itself. There are approximately four chest spawn locations in the maze and the fort of the woods, and you can quickly find them all by running around. Two usually spawn in the fort with two other chests throughout the maze itself.

To get started in Wailing Woods, drop down into the maze, pick off as many chests as you can, and then head off into the woods to build up your material stockpile before going to the center of the storm. This is a good starting strategy and will help you get going in the game without putting yourself in too much danger.

If there are others at the fort in the maze already, you can head out into the maze itself to look for chests, or you can head northwest of the fort out of the woods for another dense pack of chests just outside the tree line itself and more loot opportunities.

⑦ MOISTY MIRE

Moisty Mire is an excellent location for new players to start at because it usually has few enemies dropping down, there are quite a few chest locations and there are plenty of massive trees for you to chop down. A quick run through this swampy location can net you hundreds of wood and a few decent weapons and shield consumables as well, giving you everything that you need to go out and battle enemy players.

When you drop down in Moisty Mire it's best to look for the largest trees on the map. These large trees will have the most chests and there are a few locations right at the center of the dark green sections on the map that have the most chests overall. One of those sections features a massive tree with two chests down at its base, and the other features a tree fort with multiple levels and two chests hidden within it. If you are dropping at these key spots in Moisty Mire you should have no trouble grabbing some excellent loot.

Once you have your loot, don't waste any time chopping down some of those massive trees and heading straight in for the circle. If you wait too long you are in danger of getting stuck out in the storm. Moisty Mire is on the edge of the map and usually quite a ways away from the Eye of the Storm. That's why it's such a safe starting location, but you should expect to do some running after dropping there.

Aggressive Starting Locations

These starting locations are for more advanced players that aren't afraid to get their hands dirty. There will be lots of fighting, but if you come out on top you're going to end up with all the loot that you need to push through to be the winner of the entire game. Many of the most skilled players choose these intense starting locations for that very reason. Are you up for the challenge?

⑧ TILTED TOWERS

If you're looking for some action, this is the place to get it. A huge portion of players drop down into Tilted Towers at the beginning of every single match. That means this place turns into an all-out warzone every single game and it's a fun area to test your skills and learn combat tactics that are going to help you become more skilled than other players in the game.

Tilted Towers is literally packed with chests, so just run around scooping up loot as you go and taking out any enemies that you get a chance to attack. Try to make smart moves, use your building and shooting skills to stay ahead of your enemies and you might make it out with a good pile of loot to help you through the rest of the game.

PLEASANT PARK

Pleasant Park is well-known for its legendary level of loot and tons of chest spawns. For this reason, this location literally floods with players at the start of most matches. It's located between Haunted Hills and Loot Lake and it's a fun place to drop down on if you're looking for a challenge. It's similar to Tilted Towers, though a bit easier for less skilled players when comparing the two.

To start off your loot grab at Pleasant Park drop down to the roof or balcony of one of the corner houses and scramble for a gun as quickly as possible. Be listening closely for enemies as you move around the first house and scoop up all the loot. Once you've cleaned out your first house, and hopefully found at least one chest, build over to the roof of the next house and follow the same process. Continue this strategy through the different houses in the park, cleaning out the enemies as you go. This strategy takes some time, but should net you some decent kills and excellent loot by the time you are finished making your way through the park.

A Basic Weapons Guide

Weapons are everything in Fortnite and it's vital that you understand the many different types and how to use them most effectively as well. Read through and learn about each type of weapon and what they're good for, and then when you play you can decide on the weapon combination that you like the best.

Weapon Types

There are a wide range of weapons in Fortnite, with each having its strengths and weaknesses. Learn about the different options and you can decide what weapons you want to use during battle.

◎ SHORT RANGE

SHOTGUNS: These short-range weapons come in pump or tactical varieties. They scatter bullets in a large circle pattern and deliver a huge amount of damage to opponents nearby. Pump shotguns fire one round at a time and deliver maximum damage. Tactical shotguns can fire up to seven rounds in quick succession and deliver a lower amount of damage.

PISTOLS: These versatile short-range weapons deliver damage with light bullets. There are slow-firing high damage pistols like the revolver and hand cannon, and fast-firing low

damage versions like the standard pistol and the suppressed pistol. Both the revolver and hand-cannon are best when used for landing head-shots and for fighting a bit farther back. The suppressed and standard pistols are used right up on top of enemies instead of shotguns, especially at the beginning of a match. The standard pistol does 23-25 body damage and 46-50 head damage, while the suppressed does 26-28 body damage and 52-56 head damage which means that several shots are necessary for a kill, even to the head. The revolver on the other hand does 54-60 body damage and 108-120 head damage, while the hand cannon does 75-78 body damage and 150-156 head damage, making one shot kills possible in some situations.

CROSSBOWS: Crossbows, though currently out of Fortnite were a powerful mid-range weapon with unlimited ammunition. These weapons came in rare and epic versions and gave players the ability to fire round after round without worrying about running out of ammo. Crossbows were recently taken out of the game or "Vaulted" as they call it at Epic Games, which means they could be added back into the game in the future, but there is no guarantee that they will.

⑩ MID RANGE

SMGS: SMGs deliver short to mid-range damage effectively by firing many bullets in a straight line. They have magazines between 30 and 35 bullets overall and can be silenced for stealth attacks. Though standard SMGs were recently vaulted, tactical and suppressed SMGs still remain in the game and drop regularly.

MINIGUNS: When it comes to mid-range battles there's something reassuring about wielding the powerful minigun. The standard Minigun has an unlimited magazine and fires low damage bullets at an impressive velocity, but it takes nearly 5 seconds to get started.

ASSAULT RIFLES: These are one of the best mid-ranged weapons for precision shooting. They come with magazines of 20 to 30 bullets and deliver lots of low damage hits. Be careful not to exhaust a clip too fast, because they take between 2 and 3 seconds to reload once out.

GRENADES: Fortnite offers players a range of grenade-type weapons to attack their opponents with. There are five different types of grenades, giving you a range of attack options to work with. Standard grenades can be tossed and bounced around the ground in a map. They deliver 105 damage when tossed within range. Impulse grenades can be used to launch opponents or yourself into the air, but don't do any damage when they go off. Boogie Bombs will force your opponent to stand in place and dance, giving you

a chance to run or to take them out while they are occupied. Clinger grenades stick to enemies and deliver 105 damage to them. Remote explosives can be placed in a remote position and detonated later on for 70 damage.

⑪ LONG RANGE

SNIPER RIFLES: These long-range weapons are one of the most lethal tools in the game and a favorite for highly skilled players looking to raise their kill count. They come in a few different types though. There's the Bolt Action, the Hunting Rifle and the Semi-Automatic. The Bolt Action delivers the most damage with between 105 and 116 damage per round depending on its rarity color, but it's also the slowest to reload and only offers a single shot per magazine making it very important to land your shot. The Hunting Rifle works similarly to the Bolt Action with just a single round magazine, but the shots are less lethal with between 86 and 90 damage, and the reload time is faster. Finally there's the semi-auto rifle with a magazine size of 10 and damage in the 60's per shot. This gun has a slower firing rate, but gives you a bunch of chances to land your shot.

ROCKET LAUNCHERS: Rocket launchers are one of the most useful long range weapons in Fortnite. They travel through the air slowly, but deliver massive amounts of damage upon impact. Rockets can tear through structures and are highly effective for breaking down walls and exposing your enemies. They also deliver lethal amounts of damage when aimed at the enemy.

Understanding Rarity

There are five weapon rarities in Fortnite going from Gray to Gold. Each step up in rarity results in a more powerful and effective weapon. As you loot items you'll notice a range of weapon colors floating around, and it's important to know which ones you should be picking up and which you should ignore. The color list down below goes from the worst weapons to the best ones. As you're picking up weapons you should throw out lower quality options in favor of the higher quality ones.

GRAY ≫ GREEN ≫ BLUE ≫ PURPLE ≫ ORANGE

Gray weapons are common weapons and easiest to find, and also weakest of the bunch. Green are uncommon, and still quite easy to locate, though slightly improved over the gray ones. Blue weapons are rare, more difficult to find and quite lethal. Purple weapons are epic, and very difficult to find and offer the second highest damage output. Orange weapons

are legendary, they are the most difficult to find and also deliver the highest level of damage in the game.

As weapon rarity goes up the damage output per shot increases and the reload speed improves as well. This means that the rarest weapons in the game can deliver higher rates of sustained damage. Often weapon rarity isn't that important to winning fights though. Take for instance green versus blue pump shotguns. Both weapons will take three body shots to kill a fully shielded opponent or two head shots. Differences between rarities are often so small that they mean very little when comparing one to the other, and it's much better to look for different types of weapons instead. For instance, pump shotguns deliver higher levels of damage than tactical shotguns and bolt-action sniper rifles deliver better burst damage than semi-automatic sniper rifles.

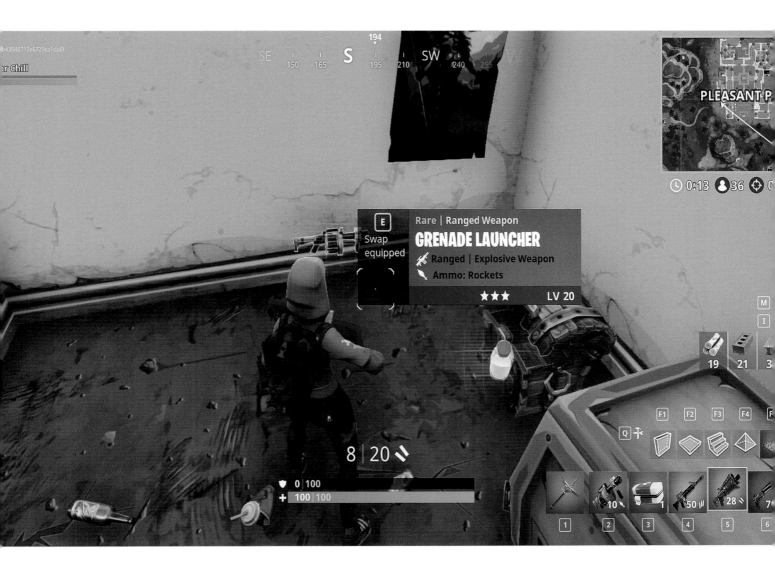

Learn the differences between individual weapon types and you'll know which weapons will help you be most effective during combat, though it's still helpful to know which color weapon you should pick.

A SOLID WEAPON LOADOUT

Your weapon loadout in Fortnite determines what tools you have at your disposal during battle, and it's crucial for success throughout a match. While there are different loadouts that work best for different scenarios, it's a good idea to learn a good solid general purpose weapon setup when starting out in the game. Here is our favorite loadout setup and it's a good idea to build something similar when new to the game.

SLOT 1: ASSAULT RIFLE
SLOT 2: SHOTGUN
SLOT 3: LONG RANGE SNIPER
SLOT 4: EXPLOSIVE WEAPON
SLOT 5: SHIELD POTIONS OR CHUG JUGS

This weapon and consumable combination is ideal for all-around play in Fortnite because it gives you tools for every situation. For close range you have the shotgun, for mid-range you have the assault rifle and you have a sniper for long range combat. If your enemy is hiding in a base your explosive weapon will make quick work of it, and the shield item will ensure that you are always protected during combat. Small shields are the best option for slot 5 because of how fast you can apply them, but any shield or Chug Jug will work as well.

Understanding Consumables

Consumables are extremely important in Fortnite, though many new players don't take them as seriously as they do the weapons. Without consumables you'll die rapidly to the first few attackers that you come into contact with. That's because you won't be able to build up a shield for extra protection, and you won't be able to recover health and shield that's lost during combat. Without consumables even experienced players would only survive a few battles in the game, which is why they must be emphasized during every match.

We're going to do a good overview of the major consumables that you'll find in Fortnite so you know what to look for, what each item is going to do for you and why you should be picking them up.

Raising Health

Health is the most important resource that you have in Fortnite. Without enough of it you'll die in one or two shots from even a weak weapon. That's why it's important to keep your eye open for consumables that will help raise your health up while in combat. Below are the most common consumables for just raising health, though there are some for health and shield combined together.

BANDAGES: Bandages are the most basic tool at your disposal for healing up your health. Each one raises health by 15 HP and works in 4 seconds. You can use bandages to raise health up to 75 HP, but can't go any higher than that without help from a different consumable.

MED KIT: The med kit is the most powerful tool for healing up health quickly, but it also takes quite a long time to use. The kit will raise your health all the way up to 100 HP, no matter what you are at. The kit takes a full 10 seconds to use though, making it a no-go in serious combat situations.

Raising Shield

Shield is arguably the most important stat to work on raising in Fortnite, especially early in the game when you are at full health. The items below all raise shield up exclusively and should be used whenever you find them and your shield is low.

⑫ SMALL SHIELD POTIONS

Small shield potions come in packs of three and can be stacked up to 10 in one slot. These potions raise your shield by up to 25, but they won't raise your shield above 50. These are the most common shields that you'll find on the map in Fortnite, and are excellent for carrying around in between matches because they take just 2 seconds to consume.

LARGE SHIELD POTIONS

Large shield potions are a rare item and much more difficult to find than small shields are. This item will raise your shield by up to 50 and can raise your shield all the way to 100. These potions take 5 seconds to consume and are much less effective in the heat of battle than the small shields are for this reason. They work well alongside small shields to raise your shield up to 100 if you take one after using two small shield potions.

SHIELD MUSHROOMS

Blue mushrooms found in the woods will raise your shield level up to 5. While these are pretty insignificant on their own, if you pick these up as you walk through the woods you can easily raise your shield by 20 or more before you get into combat once again.

HEALTH AND SHIELD COMBINATION

These combination items will raise both your shield and your health up at the same time and are helpful for getting back to a respectable health level.

⑬ SLURP JUICE

This basic liquid will raise your shield and your health by 25 each over time. It takes awhile to raise these stats all the way, so is best used outside of combat or alongside other shield and health items when you're about to get into a fight.

CHUG JUG

This ultimate consumable will raise both your shield and your health all the way to 100 regardless of what they are at before using it. This consumable takes a whopping 15 seconds to use, so make sure you are walled in and hidden well before you begin.

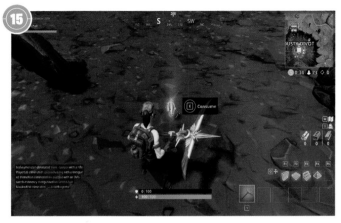

Camouflage and Protection

While shield and health are essential to winning in Fortnite, they aren't the only two things that you should be thinking about while playing the game. You should also be thinking about camouflage and protection. That's where these useful consumables come into play and they can also make a huge difference for you when used properly.

THE BUSH

This bush consumable will transform your character into a walking bush. With this item equipped you can move around the map stealthily and pick off your enemies without them knowing quite where you are located. It takes 3.5 seconds to activate, so you will want to hide until you have it fully deployed. You can attack enemies while within the Bush, but will be exposed temporarily. Be careful not to take damage while in the disguise or you will lose it and have to survive without the convenient costume.

PORT-A-FORT

The Port-a-Fort is a newer object in the Fortnite world that is a base in a ball. You just toss it out in front of you when taking fire and a large base will spring up right in front of you. The base features metal walls and a good funnel shaped perch that you can fire down on targets from. It's convenient for players that don't know how to build bases quickly, or for advanced players that want a more resilient base to fight from in a pinch.

Mobility

Moving quickly in Fortnite means being more difficult to shoot, it also means getting from one safe location to another or hunting down fleeing enemies more effectively. Hop rocks are a unique consumable that will help increase your movement capabilities while in matches.

HOP ROCKS

Dusty Depot was transformed into Dusty Divot after a huge meteor struck the world of Fortnite and what was left behind were a collection of hop rocks. These small bits of meteor are consumables that will turn your character into a bit of a superhero for the next 30 seconds. Use the rocks and you'll be jumping higher and moving more easily around obstructions as a result. The rocks will make it easier for you to locate your enemies and also to avoid taking shots from enemy players.

If you're looking for a way to improve your game, consider making more use of consumables with every match that you enter into, and save one slot for important consumables to carry around with you such as shield potions.

Basic Gathering and Crafting

Gathering is vital in every match of Fortnite or you run the risk of leaving yourself without the ability to build ramps, walls and other defenses against your enemies. From the start of a match you should begin hammering away at trees, cars, pallets, containers and all the other resources around you in the match. It's important that you gather whenever you have the chance, or you could end up getting trapped or not having a way to protect yourself, which is a guaranteed death.

⑯ HIT THE SWEET SPOT

Whenever you're gathering in Fortnite, make sure you aim your pickaxe for the small circle that pops up on the resource. Hitting the circle does double damage and will really bring in materials quickly. This is the trick that players use to get resources faster and to get through buildings before their enemies do. If you stand back from an object while gathering you might have some difficulty hitting the circle every single time. There's a trick to enhance your accuracy though. Stand right on top of the object as close as you can possibly get. Most of the time the circle will remain in your direct aim and you'll hit it again and again gathering resources lightning fast.

FOCUS ON WOOD

Though wood is the weakest of all the materials, it's also the quickest and easiest to gather. Start off building a supply of wood, because you can grab it fast and once you have a few hundred you'll be able to build ramps, forts and other complex structures to help you stay alive. Focus on pallets and trees when gathering wood for best results.

⑰ PICK UP THE RESOURCE BLOCKS

As you loot in Fortnite you'll notice small resource blocks that are located in houses and in other areas of the map. Always grab these if you can because they will give you 30 of that particular resource, helping you build up your supply quickly.

RELY ON YOUR ENEMIES

It's always a good idea to keep materials stockpiled for a battle, but unless you are going to be climbing to the top of the map with something like the Stairway to Heaven strategy, you probably won't need hundreds and hundreds of materials. Instead stock up a few hundred and focus on beating your competitors. Each time you take out an enemy you'll acquire all their resources, making it easy to keep stocked up once you go into battle.

Comparing Materials

There are three different materials that you have to work with for any building project, wood, brick and metal, and it's important to know which are the most valuable and which you should skip over when doing early game gathering.

⑱ WOOD IS PERFECT FOR FAST DEFENSE

Wooden structures are the weakest of all the materials when they are fully built, but they are the strongest when you first lay them down. If you put down a wooden wall and a metal wall to block a shot, the wooden wall will hold up better when attacked immediately. It takes roughly 6.8 seconds before the metal wall becomes more effective defensively than wood. Wood is also more effective than brick for fast defense. That's why when you're under fire you should be laying down wooden walls for protection every single time. Always make sure you have some wood stocked up, because it's your number one defensive shield.

METAL IS BEST FOR LONG TERM BASES

Even though wood is best when throwing up defenses fast, metal is much better for constructing a durable base when you have some time on your hands. Once completely built up metal walls offer a stunning 400 HP while wood offers just 200 HP and brick offers 300 HP. That means that whenever you're setting up a base and you aren't under immediate attack, metal is the way to go. Metal is also a helpful material for the top of sniper towers and lookouts, because characters blend in better with metal than they do with wood.

BRICK IS ALWAYS SECOND BEST

Brick is the least valuable resource in the game because it's not really good at anything. It offers less immediate defense with just 90 HP compared to 100 HP offered by wood, and it offers less long-term durability than metal with a max of 300 HP compared to 400. That doesn't mean that you shouldn't use brick if you have it, it just means that you shouldn't work hard to acquire the resource. If you're out of wood, brick makes the best quick protection. If you're out of metal, brick is better for long-term bases than wood is. Use it when necessary, but rely on the more effective resources when you have them available in the game.

Simple Structures

We cover much more advanced building projects in the Advanced Building chapter section of this book, but to give new players something to work with when first starting off, we're going to explain a few basic structures that they can use.

⑲ PANIC WALLS

Panic walls are as simple as they sound. They are just a simple wall placed in between you and a firing enemy. Lay down a single wood wall for the most durable shield and move away from your enemy, or toss a ramp behind the wall to give you the height advantage and a place to shoot down from.

Even new players should be using panic walls all the time, so get used to building when you are in trouble to help your character survive more effectively.

SAFETY BOX

The Safety Box is another very simple structure that can save your life in heated combat. To make it simply hold the build button on a wall and spin your character in a full circle. You will put a box around your character effectively stopping damage from every side at once. This is perfect for situations when you are being sniped, or for times when you just want to heal up a bit.

⑳ ONE RAMP FORT

The one ramp fort is a variation on the standard Safety Box. You make a box around your character and then jump while facing the direction of your enemy and laying a ramp down below you. You will end up on top of the ramp with the highest point in the direction of your enemy. Climb the

ramp and fire down at the enemy from up above. This can be enhanced by making multiple boxes on top of the first and adding a ramp each time, and that's exactly how a sniper tower is formed!

TWO RAMP FORT

Just like the simple one ramp fort, the two ramp fort is very simple to make. Create a box around your character, only this time make the side that's facing your enemies two walls long instead of one. With your rectangular structure you are ready to add two ramps. Add your ramps both facing the direction of the shooter side by side, or make the ramps facing away from one another with the low end in the middle of the box and the high end out at the edges. This gives you space for you and another player to climb up and attack enemies that are coming your way, and this structure is very simple to create.

㉑ EDITING IN A DOOR

With any of the box structures you should think about editing in a door to the back of the space. This gives you a quick escape and ensures that you aren't caught when enemies start breaking through. To do this just press "G" on PC, hold "B" on an Xbox controller or hold "Circle" on the PS4 controller while facing the wall that you want to edit. Now remove two boxes stacked on top of one another starting at the bottom and going up. This will put a door in that location of the wall.

Getting Good

The number one question that new players ask us is how can they get good at the game? They want us to tell them a secret that will make them better than other players, and other than basic tactics the only secret is practice. You need to practice the game to get good at it, and more time practicing will result in more skill. That doesn't mean that you should just load the game up over and over and play without any strategy behind your practice though. That's why we've put together some basic strategies, practice scenarios and tips to help you develop your skill and practice your way to the top.

Learning to Shoot and Survive

Understanding how to shoot effectively and how to survive heated combat are the two most important skills in Fortnite that you should focus on developing. This is especially true when you are in the early stages of learning the game. Later on you can focus on things like enhancing your building skills, but knowing how to build well won't do you any good if you can't at least lock onto your enemy with a weapon.

㉒ THE POPULATED AREA TRAINING STRATEGY

Getting good at fighting is the first thing that you should focus on in Fortnite, and it's difficult to learn without lots of practice. That's why we recommend the populated area training strategy to new players. This is a bit like throwing yourself to the wolves, but it's a powerful training tool when done right. Fly down to populated sections of the map by dropping down as fast as you can at the beginning of a match and try to grab a weapon and get eliminations immediately.

By doing this over and over again you'll learn how to outsmart opponents, you'll learn how to aim effectively and to eliminate players. Dozens of speed rounds in this fashion will help you hone your skills and get comfortable going up against other players without worrying about dying so much. Not only that, but speed running like this is a lot of fun and who doesn't like getting eliminations?

UTILIZING LOBBY TIME

The lobby isn't just a waiting area to get the game started, it's a training tool as well. Pick up those weapons and practice landing headshots on people walking around. Grab the materials that you see and try to throw up a basic fort fast. Those short lobby waits can help you improve your game, so make sure you're using them as much as you can.

㉓ DOUBLE SHOTGUNS: FIRE OFF MORE SHOTS FASTER WHILE MASTERING PUMP

Fighting with shotguns is one of the more difficult skills to master. To be effective you need to be able to swivel your view quickly and lock on to your opponent with precision. We always recommend the pump shotgun to skilled shooters, but when first building your skill we recommend a modified setup to players. Instead of going with a single pump shotgun, use a pump shotgun and then a pump or a tactical shotgun in the next slot. When fighting fire off that single pump round and quickly swap to the second shotgun to finish off your opponent. Once you get good enough to land pump shotgun headshots almost every time, you won't need this strategy any longer. Until then, it's a good idea to carry two shotguns.

㉔ BUILD THEN SHOOT STRATEGY

Most players that are new to Fortnite get better at aiming, but rarely improve on their buildings. That's because aiming is intuitive to any gamer that's familiar with shooters, so it's the more comfortable skill. If you find yourself having trouble building, the only way to improve the skill is to force yourself to do it.

We've put together this unique challenge to help you improve your skills with building. The idea is simple. At the beginning of the match gather plenty of materials. Then each time you encounter someone, you need to build a basic structure before you can shoot them. That means lay down a wall, toss down a ramp, climb into position and then start firing! This will be frustrating at first and you'll die many times, but eventually you'll see that building gives you a real advantage and you'll find it easier to pick off your opponents from within your small base. You'll also notice that you're getting more comfortable with building structures quickly. Once you're comfortable with building simple structures fast, you can move on from this challenge and know that you succeeded.

Learning to Build Effectively

Building isn't a natural skill when you first begin playing Fortnite, which is why it takes time to develop. Our top recommendation for learning to build well is to choose a starting location that's at the edge of the map and just gather and focus on building basic structures. The woods around Lonely Lodge is a perfect spot for this sort of skill building activity. Spend enough time putting up forts, sniper towers and other structures and you'll get comfortable building quickly. Try to learn to switch from one building block to the next without having to think about it. Just a few rounds of this type of practice and you'll be much more comfortable with building.

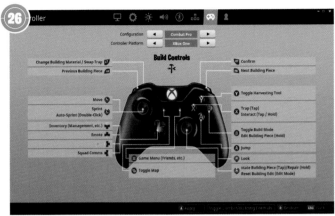

Optimizing Your Character

Optimizing your character in Fortnite means getting weapons where you know how to access them quickly, setting your look sensitivity to a level that lets you aim effectively and choosing controls that you are comfortable with. When you take the time to set up your character to play as effectively as possible, you set yourself up for success in combat. If you can't be bothered to optimize these sort of things, you're going to struggle more when you try to improve your game.

25 SET WEAPON ORDER

While playing Fortnite it's best to try and pick up the same type of weapons each time that you play a round and to put them into similar locations as well. If you do this regularly you should know exactly where your shotgun is, where your assault rifle is, where your sniper is and where any other objects are in the heat of combat. It's extremely helpful to be able to switch from one weapon type to another rapidly while battling so that you can use combat strategies to help you win fights. For instance, if you are sniping an enemy and you hit a solid body shot that weakens your opponent, your best option is often to switch to an assault rifle to finish off your target. This works well if you switch fast, but if you go too slow you will miss your chance.

To make sure you don't have this issue when battling enemies in Fortnite, put the guns you use most often in specific slots on your character. Press "I" on PC or D-Pad up on Xbox One or the track pad on the PS4 controller to open up the inventory. Once opened arrange the different weapons that you use regularly into specific locations. With your shotgun in the first slot, the assault rifle in the second slot and a sniper in the third slot you will always know how to quickly switch from one weapon to another in fast combat, which is an important optimization.

26 CHANGE YOUR CONTROLS

Fortnite comes with different control loadouts that you can pick and choose from. When you are first getting started with the game it can be overwhelming trying to learn all the different controls that you have to use. Before you take the time to learn all those different controls, take a look at the different custom options available to you. Choose an option with controls that you like the best and go with that setup. The custom options might be more comfortable for you than the standard controls are, which is important in a fast-paced game like Fortnite.

ADJUST LOOK SENSITIVITY

Finally you should look into changing around the look sensitivity of your character. On PC that means adjusting your mouse sensitivity to an amount that feels comfortable. On PS4 or Xbox One it means adjusting the sensitivity of the thumb stick that handles moving your view around. Go up to a higher

sensitivity to turn faster, or lower your sensitivity for more accurate aiming. A higher sensitivity is generally more effective at close range, while a lower sensitivity has a slight advantage at range. Your best option is to adjust the sensitivity around and play matches to fine-tune what feels best to you.

Quick Tips to Play Better

These simple tips should help improve your success in Fortnite at least to a slight degree. Keep them in mind when you play and try to use at least one or two of them each time that you go into combat. By utilizing these tips you'll play more effectively and have greater success in Fortnite overall.

㉗ FOCUS THE HEAD

Heashots are incredibly powerful in Fortnite and will allow you to take out opponents much more quickly than body shots. Always aim at your opponent's upper torso in hopes of getting a mix of head and body shots while in combat. This mix will help you avoid missing too often, but will also increase your total damage output nicely.

SLIDE SAFELY

If you're climbing down a hill and you don't want to take damage, just hold the back arrow while going down or push your joystick back toward the hill and you'll safely slide all the way down. This only works with cliffs that don't drop off straight down though, so be careful when using this tactic.

PLATFORM DOWN

If you're going off a sheer cliff and you think you could fall to your death, have no fear, use platforms to get down to safety. Just build platforms underneath your character on the side of the cliff edge. They will serve as steps that you can climb down on and help you safely get down to the ground.

RIDE SUPPLY DROPS

Getting supply drops is incredibly difficult with so many other players also going for them. One way to gain early access to these loot crates is to take a launch pad up into the air to get you on top of a supply drop. When you do this you can start looting it earlier and you are more difficult to pick off than you would be if you tried to loot the box down on the ground.

BUILD THEN SHOOT

The number one tip for new players is that they need to build and then shoot at enemies. Build a ramp, toss down some walls and climb up top for added protection while shooting at enemies as fast as possible. This gives you cover if you start to take too much damage, and gives you a better vantage point to fire from as well.

㉘ GO FOR ENHANCED AIM

With weapons like the sniper rifle or the revolver it's important to stop and maybe even crouch for a second before shooting. This enhances your character's aim to help ensure you get the most accurate shot. Don't just hold the shoot button down with your weapon or you run the risk of missing many of your shots and wasting your ammo in a fight.

SNEAK THEN SHOOT

Generally, it's a bad idea to shoot at an enemy as soon as you see them, unless they are quite close to you and they don't know where you are just yet. Instead, sneak up closer to the enemy, toss down a quick fort and let them have it. Taking the time to get closer to your enemy will make sure that those first few shots hit the mark, otherwise you run the risk of missing and giving away your position at the same time.

LAND QUICKLY

Jump from the Battle Bus as close to your final destination as possible and then aim your character straight down into a dive so you get to the location as quickly as you can. Getting to the ground fast means getting the loot before your enemies do, and that's a very good thing.

Leveling Your Character

Whether you just want to brag to your friends about how high your character level is, or you want the Tier stars that come along with those levels to help you level up toward the in-game items more effectively, it's important to understand how to level your character in Fortnite as efficiently as possible.

GAINING LEVELS EFFECTIVELY

While in battle in Fortnite there are a few different things that you can do to level up as quickly as possible. The first is survive for as long as you can. The higher your position is in a particular match, the more experience you'll get at the end of it all. That's a good reason to do your best not to die right away, especially if you aren't going to get a few kills on your way to death. Play safe, don't spawn in heavily populated locations and you should have no trouble lasting for a long time before you are taken out.

The next step is to kill off players and do damage whenever you can. For every elimination that you get during a match you're going to get a nice boost of experience that will help you level up your character more quickly. Get a few kills during the match and you'll notice a nice experience boost. Also, open chests and ammo crates whenever you can during a match, even if you have all the loot that you need already. This will increase your total experience at the end of the match. It's also a good idea to play with friends whenever possible, because doing so gives you a pretty generous experience boost as well.

Finally, you should do your best to win matches. I know, it's easier said than done, but winning a match will reward you with a handsome experience bonus. Do your best to win matches by fighting for survival and working hard to eliminate opponents and you'll get some serious experience at the end of each match.

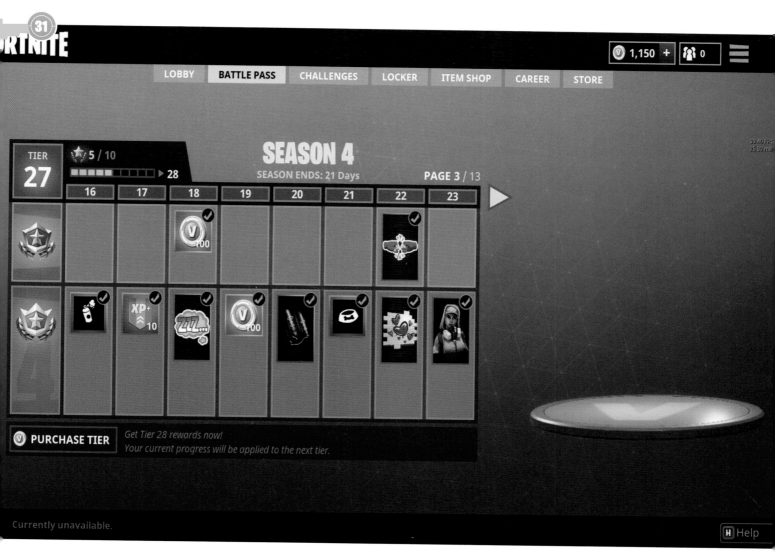

③ USING EXPERIENCE BOOSTS

Playing carefully to survive as long as possible in matches, and fighting for eliminations are two steps to help you level up as quickly as possible, but you'll level even faster with some help from experience boosts. If you have the Fortnite Battle pass you can gain access to serious experience boosts by getting Battle Stars and climbing up through the tiers. Exp boosts will help you level faster and will in turn help your Tier level increase as well which is good for your Fortnite career.

Gaining levels isn't all that difficult in Fortnite, and just getting into matches and doing your best is all you should have to do in order to level your character up and gain those precious Battle Stars that come along with level gains.

Understanding Fortnite Tiers

At the beginning of each new season in Fortnite a new Battle Pass is released. This is a progression track that players are supposed to work through as they play the game. There is a free progression track and a paid progression track. Players that pay 950 V-Bucks can purchase the Battle Pass for that season and enjoy a bunch of perks along with their purchase. The major perk of the Battle Pass is access to exclusive premium items for reaching different tier levels in the game, but the Battle Pass also includes additional challenges and experience boosts to make leveling and tiering up easier.

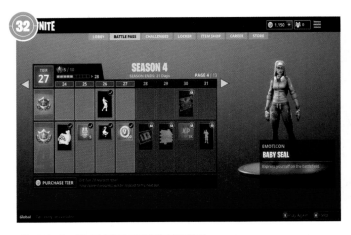

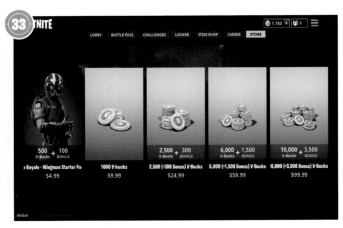

³² GAINING TIERS EFFICIENTLY

Tiers in Fortnite are the more important levels that you should be trying to gain. There are 100 tiers per season Battle Pass, and by gaining all 100 tiers you'll unlock a bunch of exclusive items, V-bucks and special boosts that help increase your rewards as you play.

There are two different ways for you to gain tiers as a player in Fortnite. The first is by leveling up your character. The second is by completing challenges for the game. Every tier level requires 10 Battle Stars, and your character will earn Battle Stars each time they level up. For any level that doesn't end in 5 or 0 the player will earn a single Battle Star for leveling up. For levels that end in 5 the player will receive 5 Battle Stars for leveling up, and for levels that end in 0, the player will receive 10 Battle Stars or a full tier for leveling up. All the free Battle Stars offered is exactly why it's so important to try and level up your Fortnite character as much as possible while playing the game.

While leveling your character you should also be actively completing challenges in the game. This includes everything from solving treasure maps, to finding letters, to killing enemies, to surviving longer than your enemies. There are daily challenges for free players, and season weekly challenges for premium Battle Pass holders. These challenges all pay out a set amount of Battle Stars, usually 5 or 10, and help you raise your tier level up closer to 100. If you're serious about the game and you want to get as many of the items

offered as possible, it makes sense to work to complete the different tier levels of the Battle Pass every single season, plus it gives you a goal to work toward as you play.

Using V-Bucks

V-Bucks are the currency in Fortnite and they are a tool for you to get additional perks and customizations for your character. There are three major ways for you to use V-Bucks while playing Fortnite and each one benefits your character and you in some way, but before we even worry about how to use V-Bucks we should cover how to get them in the first place. Read on and learn where this currency comes from.

³³ GETTING V-BUCKS

The most direct way to get V-Bucks is to purchase them from Epic Games directly. It doesn't matter if you play on PC, Xbox One or PS4, you can easily buy V-Bucks from the marketplace that's tied to your system. V-Bucks cost around $10 per 1,000 that you purchase, though you get bonus V-Bucks when you purchase them in larger packages. You must purchase a minimum of $10 worth when buying them from the marketplace.

If you don't want to purchase V-Bucks you can also unlock them through the game's Battle Pass. Both the free and premium tracks of the pass come with V-Buck rewards for leveling up. Just complete challenges, level up and you'll unlock a bunch of V-Bucks for free.

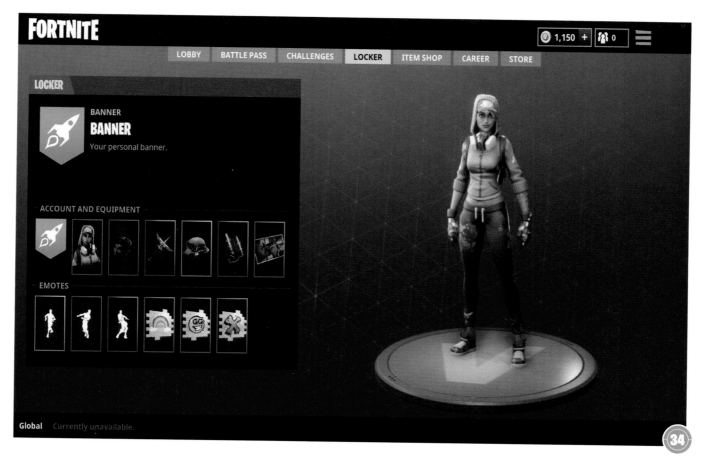

CUSTOMIZING YOUR CHARACTER

Once you have V-Bucks you can use them directly in the items shop to customize your character. Purchase skins, emotes, back bling, pickaxes, gliders and trails to make your character look exactly the way you want them to while in the game. Many of these items cost hundreds of V-Bucks and some cost thousands so make sure that you purchase enough to get all the customizations you are interested in. The item store changes on a daily basis, so if you don't see an item that you want check back again another time.

㉞ GETTING THE BATTLE PASS

V-Bucks are the only way for you to purchase the Battle Pass in Fortnite as well. Get a 1,000 pack and you can purchase the Battle Pass with 50 V-Bucks to spare. Once you have the pass you can start playing through it and unlock some free V-Bucks for your character. The pass is affordable when you consider all the content that it unlocks for the game, and it will make playing more fun and give you more goals to shoot for with each Fortnite session that you go through.

BUYING TIERS

Finally, V-Bucks can be used to purchase tiers of the Battle Pass. Whether you are just having difficulty leveling yourself up through the pass, or you want to get to the later game items quickly, you can easily purchase tiers and move up to the higher levels of your Battle Pass in less time. Doing this makes it easier to unlock the hard to reach items of the pass, and will give you a head start on the competition so you can grab the customizations and boosts before them.

Hopefully this getting started guide has helped you figure out how to begin with Fortnite. From here we focus on more in-depth help for different aspects of the game, including using weapons, building advanced structures, customizing your character to the fullest extent and getting as much as possible out of the Fortnite Battle Pass. I encourage you to look through any of the following sections that match what you want to get out of the game most next and to jump around the book to help you get as much as possible out of every session with Fortnite. ★

The Complete Weapons Guide

OTHER THAN MAYBE BUILDING, MASTERING WEAPONS IS THE MOST IMPORTANT SKILL TO DEVELOP IN FORTNITE.
Not only do you need to know how the different weapons work, and where to find them, but you need to know which weapons you should be using depending on the situation that you are in. There's a wide selection of weapons in the game, and if you aren't sure which ones are worth picking up, you're going to be very confused and miss out on opportunities to overtake your enemies. That's why it makes sense to read through our complete weapons guide, so that you know exactly what to expect and how to gain the edge over each opponent that you face up against. It will take some time to get through, but once you've made it through our guide you'll be comfortable grabbing loot and you'll be ready to start fighting for first place.

The guide will explain what each of the different weapon types are and how they should be used in combat. It will help you understand why the guns are different colors, and which colors you should be picking up and which ones you should be swapping out. The guide will give you some ideal weapon loadouts to work with, it will explain some of the other attack accessories like grenades, and will give you some advanced tactics to try out in the heat of combat. Between all these different bits of advice you should feel comfortable handling all the weapons in the game, and more importantly, you should know how to make the most of them to overcome your opponents when doing so means the most.

The Different Weapon Types

There are six main types of weapons in Fortnite, and each type is good for something else. As a player looking to improve and make the most of the game, you should know about each weapon type and which one is right for your current situation. As you explore the world and loot locations you'll find some of each of these weapon types, and before you know it you'll be creating weapon combinations that you believe will help you overwhelm the other players you are tasked with beating.

SMGs

SMGs or submachine guns are a powerful close to mid-range firing option in Fortnite. They come in three different styles currently and can be used to deliver a huge amount of damage when operated properly.

TACTICAL SMGS

With the basic SMG removed from the game, tactical SMGs are the new standard option. They are loud, fire fast and do quite a bit of damage, and can be found from common to epic rarities. These guns do from 16 to 18 damage per shot and have a decent magazine size of 30 bullets so you can just keep firing during a fight. It's best to pull these out when just out of shotgun range, or when shotgun fire starts to spread out significantly. You should be able to land far more shots than your enemy can in a short period of time.

SILENT SMGS

Silenced SMGs are the weakest of all the different SMG types, but arguably the most useful of them. That's because you can start picking off an enemy without alerting others around you, and because even if you miss your first few shots it's unlikely that the enemy will even notice they are being fired on right away. The silenced SMG does between 17 and 19 damage per round, but fires considerably slower than the two other types of SMGs. It's good for close to mid-range combat situations and is very good for getting stealth kills.

MINIGUN

The minigun is a cool weapon because it can be fired continuously until it's empty. When using this weapon it's important to keep a few things in mind. The gun takes a bit of time to spin up and begin firing, so it's difficult to take out enemies with it if they get the drop on you. It is also quite loud, so it could draw the attention of other nearby enemies to your location. As long as you can work around these two drawbacks to the gun you can use it to deliver serious damage to most enemies, and it's a powerful tool for taking out multiple targets as well. Each round does between 16 and 17 damage, and you'll fire off more than 10 rounds per seconds with the gun. It can only be found in epic or legendary rarities, so you'll be looking for purple and orange guns if you want to test out the minigun.

FIGHTING WITH SMGS

You need to draw a very fine line when fighting with SMGs because they are only useful when certain conditions are met. If you're within shotgun range SMGs will only get you killed, because the shotgun can deliver damage faster in short range situations. The best time to use an SMG is just past shotgun distance when you can land most of your shots. In this situation the SMG can do more damage than most assault rifles, and will land you a great deal of kills. If you try to attack enemies that are too far away with an SMG you will often be taken out with an assault rifle though, so try and gauge the situation with care and use the right gun for the job before you begin fighting.

Pistols

Pistols are one of the most underused weapons in Fortnite and they are often passed over as soon as possible for more powerful weapons. Even so, it's vital for you to understand pistols and to know how to make the most of whatever pistol you happen to pick up early on. That's because there are going to be situations where you are stuck using a pistol to fight off enemies, and in those situations you want to come out on top of the fight, even if your enemy is wielding a shotgun.

THE STANDARD PISTOL

Standard pistols deliver between 54 and 60 damage per shot and every bit of damage they do is doubled when landed on the head. These weapons are more dangerous than most players realize and can be used to very effectively take out enemies early on in the game, but only if they are used properly. Pistols work best at close range when fired as fast as possible for a mix of head and body shots.

Pistols fire very rapidly, and can take out enemies with a handful of head shots. To make best use of a pistol fire at your enemy as fast as you can as soon as they pop up into view and try to land as many headshots as you can without compromising body shot damage. With a 16 shot magazine you shouldn't have too much trouble landing the 4 or 5 shots you need to kill your enemy.

THE REVOLVER

Revolvers are slow-firing pistols with just six bullet magazines. They fire at less than one round per second and take over two seconds to reload after you fire through your full magazine, making it very important for you to land shots accurately with this weapon. The revolver is the most difficult of all the pistols to use, and probably the last one that you want to pick up. If you do happen to get stuck with one of these weapons there are a few different ways to use them to do as much damage as possible. To effectively kill with the revolver you need to go for headshots every single time that you use it. Stop moving a second before firing a round from the revolver and consider crouching to get the highest level of accuracy from the gun and aim for the head every time. With between 54 and 60 damage per shot, headshots will always hit over 100 damage from this gun and can be used to take out players at the beginning of the game instantly.

HAND CANNON

The Desert Eagle pistol, called the hand cannon in Fortnite, is very similar to the revolver, but much more effective and worth holding onto. These weapons get an additional magazine round with 7 total shots before running out, as well as a slightly faster reload time than the revolver at 2.1 or 2.0 seconds, rather than the fastest revolver reload time of 2.2 seconds. The hand cannon really shines when you look at damage output. This gun puts out a whopping 75 or 78 damage just for body shots. That means that headshots will always do 150 or more damage with the hand cannon and that's what makes this gun so useful.

Just like with the revolver, you'll want to take maximum accuracy shots with this gun as often as possible. Landing a single headshot will take out all but the most well protected enemies. If you can deliver a headshot to an opponent you'll cut through all their shield and at least 50 health as well. From there it's best to switch over to an SMG or assault rifle to finish them off for a quick kill.

SUPPRESSED PISTOL

The suppressed pistol is one of the newer additions to Fortnite and one of the most useful pistol types that you can get. Suppressed pistols do between 26 and 28 damage for every body shot, with damage doubling to 52 to 56 damage for head shots. These guns are almost completely silent and can be used to deliver high levels of damage without drawing attention to your location. These pistols have 16 round magazines and take just 1.3 seconds to reload, making them the fastest reloading of any of the pistols.

Suppressed pistols are one of the most useful weapons in Fortnite because they are good for short range and mid-range damage. At short range they can be used to quickly overwhelm the enemy with lots of body shots and a few headshots. At long range, they maintain the accuracy level of an assault rifle, but draw much less attention to your location. This means they are perfect for picking off enemies stealthily and can help you effectively get more kills than you would with a comparable assault rifle. Suppressed

pistols also do more damage than green or blue assault rifles do when comparing the numbers, which makes them a very desirable tool to pick up. Whenever you see one of these weapons on the ground it's worth grabbing them up because you'll undoubtedly get yourself into a situation where the suppressed pistol is the perfect tool for the job.

Sniper Rifles

Sniper rifles are one of the least versatile weapons in the game, but highly useful for taking enemies out at long range. They can deliver deadly levels of damage to enemies without them even knowing where it is coming from.

HUNTING RIFLE

The hunting rifle is a non-scoped sniper that can be used to effectively kill enemies, even though it's the least desirable of all the sniping options in Fortnite. Hunting rifles deliver between 86 and 90 damage for body shots, and they deliver over 200 damage per headshot thanks to the 2.5x headshot multiplier that sniper rifles enjoy. The gun is good for mid to long-range situations and is a lethal tool when used properly in combat.

To make use of the hunting rifle properly you have two options within a fight. The first is to land a headshot and kill your enemy instantly no matter what sort of health

and shield combination they have. The second is to land a body shot and quickly switch over to an assault rifle or suppressed pistol to finish them off. Either option works, but headshots are preferable whenever you can manage to land them on your enemies.

SEMI-AUTOMATIC

The semi-automatic rifle is a rapid firing long range weapon that can be used to deliver multiple shots to enemies at range. It's much more effective at extreme distances than an assault rifle is, while still being able to deliver multiple shots of damage in short periods of time. The semi-auto rifle does between 63 and 66 damage per shot and has a 10 round magazine giving you plenty of shots to pick off your enemies with.

The semi-auto is the perfect weapon for those that are new to sniping because they will get many shots to practice compensating for leading and bullet drop, but it is more difficult to kill off enemies with for seasoned veterans that are already good at sniping. The best way to use this weapon is to go for multiple headshots as fast as possible. Enemies can be taken out with a single headshot from this rifle if they don't have a shield, if they do have a shield you'll need to land two headshots or up to four body shots in order to

remove them from the game. Make sure that you're hiding and peeking as much as possible with this rifle, and take a couple shots each time that you peek out to get more kills. It doesn't matter too much whether you are using the purple or orange semi-auto, both are just as lethal during combat.

BOLT-ACTION

The bolt-action rifle is often the favorite sniper of veteran Fortnite players because of its lethal potential. This rifle comes equipped with a long range scope, and can deliver between 105 and 110 damage per body shot or more than 200 damage per head shot. The rifle has just a single bullet magazine like the hunting rifle, but has a much longer reload time, making it very important to hide down in a fort when reloading this rifle.

The bolt-action rifle is a favorite because it can be used at extreme distances and can kill enemies in a single shot. It will take out any unshielded enemy as long as you can hit them at all, and it will take out any enemy in the game with a single shot if you can land a headshot.

To use the bolt-action effectively, get a good hiding spot, lock onto your enemy and try to land a headshot every single time. If you don't land a headshot you'll have to wait around 3 seconds before you can fire again, more than enough time for your enemy to find cover.

Shotguns

Shotguns are the go-to weapon for players in Fortnite engaging in close-range combat. That's because these guns deliver huge amounts of damage to enemies in a short period of time, and they are easy to aim at close range. There are a few different types of shotguns to choose from, but they all deliver lethal amounts of damage when used properly.

PUMP

The pump shotgun is the favorite close-range weapon for pro players and other players highly skilled at Fortnite. This weapon can deliver between 80 and 85 damage to enemies with a simple body shot when all the pellets land on the target. Pump shotguns have a 5 round magazine and have a very slow rate of fire at just 0.7 rounds per second.

The pump shotgun is such an effective weapon for two reasons. It can kill some enemies in a single shot to the head as long as they don't have maximum shield. It can also be

used to seriously weaken enemies with body shots. The pump shotgun is highly effective at longer range than other shotgun varieities because it has a tighter pellet spread than the other shotguns. The pump was recently nerfed bringing its damage down low enough to prevent it from taking out full shield enemies with a single headshot, but it's still a powerful tool against close-range enemies.

TACTICAL

The tactical shotgun is a fast-firing high damage tool for close-range combat that's ideal in some situations in the game. This shotgun has an 8 round magazine and does between 67 and 74 damage per body shot. These guns will do a minimum of 134 damage per headshot, and up to 148 damage per headshot depending on rarity. The gun has a 1.5 shots per second rate of fire, which is slightly faster than twice as fast as the pump.

Tactical shotguns are ideal tools for less skilled attackers in Fortnite because you can put out more shots in the same period of time. That means you have more chances to land your attacks. It's possible to kill off enemies with just one or two shots to the head with a tactical and between three and four body shots depending on the rarity of your tactical shotgun.

Tactical shotguns are best when used at short range and can be used to take out one or two enemies effectively. The

best strategy is to go for headshots whenever possible, but a series of body shots is better than nothing. If you are newer to the game and having trouble getting kills using the pump shotgun, start using the tactical instead and work on nailing your aim. You'll be amazed at how many kills you can get with this potent weapon, even if more experienced players decide to leave tactical shotguns behind every single time.

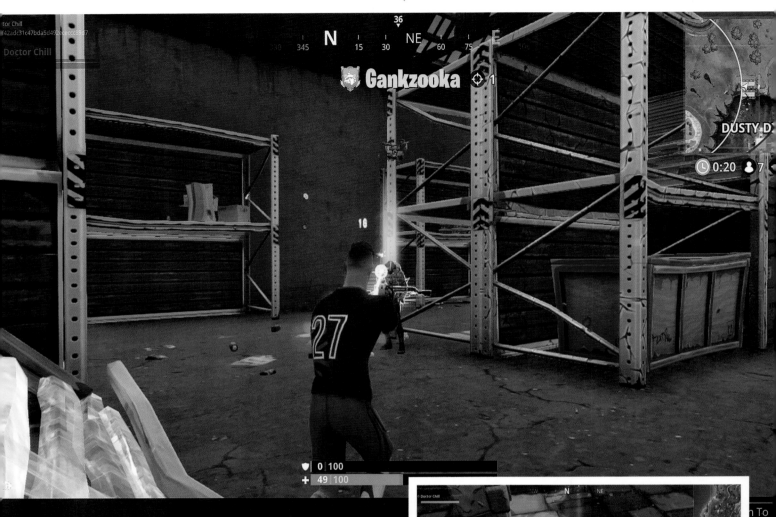

HEAVY

The heavy shotgun is a more recent addition into Fortnite and thanks to recent updates is now the most powerful shotgun in the game. This shotgun is only available in epic and legendary rarity levels or blue and purple, and delivers between 73.5 and 77 body damage when all pellets land on target. This is the only shotgun to maintain the powerful 2.5 headshot multiplier, which means it delivers between 180 and 190 damage when you land a headshot. This shotgun fires at a rate of one round per second, making it faster than the pump and slower than the tactical shotgun, and it's a seriously powerful weapon for taking enemies out at close range.

The best use for the heavy shotgun is to aim at the upper torso for headshot damage whenever in close quarters with other players. Fire off as many rounds as possible while moving around and hope for kills. The heavy shotgun is difficult to find, but it can make you really powerful at close range if you do happen to locate one.

Explosives

Explosives are a powerful tool for dealing damage to players and structures in Fortnite, but these tools are a bit more difficult to use than guns are. There is more thinking involved to really get explosives working for you properly, which is why we're going to cover the different options and how to make the most of them here. With six different varieties of explosive weapons available in the game, there are plenty of options to choose from and a lot for any player to learn before getting started.

GRENADE

Standard grenades are common and can be found all over the map. You'll find these items often and should be able to use them to take out enemies effectively with the right strategy. Grenades do 105 damage to regular enemies and 393 damage to structures.

When attacking with grenades it's best to toss them into enemy bases or down the hall or down a floor in buildings. This does two different things at the same time. It creates a serious point of damage that might hit your enemy and soften them up or even kill them. The grenade also does serious damage to the surrounding structure, and could open up a wall in your enemy's defenses so that you can start blasting away at them for serious damage.

IMPULSE GRENADE

The impulse grenade does no actual damage and instead pushes people away from it violently after going off. If an impulse grenade goes off next to you it will launch you in the direction opposite from it and potentially do damage to you if you get launched vertically. Impulse grenades are rare and more difficult to find than standard grenades are.

To best use impulse grenades you'll have to be creative. They can be used to push enemies off cliffs, to knock them off their bases, to push them into spike traps, to put some ground between you and an enemy wielding a shotgun, or even to help you launch yourself up into an enemy base or to the top of a cliff. They take a lot of practice to use and are something that you should try out whenever you get the chance.

CLINGER

The clinger is a sticky explosive that looks like a plunger. This uncommon weapon does 100 damage to people and 200 damage to structures. It's best used for taking out enemy opponents and is simple to stick to people after you get practice aiming it.

To use the clinger effectively, pop out from hiding and stick it to your opponent and then hide once again. It takes a moment to detonate, so you are better off hiding again while switching to your weapon to finish off the enemy. Once the explosive goes off, finish off your enemy with something like a shotgun, SMG or pistol.

ROCKET LAUNCHER

The rocket launcher is a favored tool by most serious Fortnite players because it's easy to aim and it does a tremendous level of damage to players and more importantly structures. Rockets from these launchers do between 110 and 121 damage to players directly and damage is much larger to structures themselves. Rocket launchers only hold a single rocket at a time, and they take about 1.6 to 1.8 seconds to reload after each shot. This makes them somewhat slow, and only useful for that first initial shot.

The best way to use a rocket launcher is to fire it off at a structure that's protecting your enemy, and to quickly switch over to a sniper or assault rifle to pick off your enemy once the wall is blown away. Don't make the mistake of firing at enemies that are too close to you with this weapon or you'll take serious damage. Also don't try to directly hit enemies with rockets if you have another gun that's appropriate for the range you're fighting at, because standard guns are more accurate and much faster than rocket launchers are.

GRENADE LAUNCHER

The grenade launcher is a bit of an odd weapon that most players prefer not to use, but it can be pretty effective at knocking out enemy players and for burning holes through their structures. This weapon comes with a 6 round magazine and grenades fire out from it one per second. It does between 100 and 105 damage depending on the rarity of the launcher, and each improved grenade launcher reloads a bit faster than the lower tiers do.

Since grenades do 100 damage to people and 200 damage to structures, grenade launchers should be targeted through the top of forts and other structures, or into windows or other openings in a base. Doing so will do serious damage to the structure while also hurting the enemy, and launching a full magazine of grenades into any location can mean death for most enemies there unless they are very quick to put up a wall or run away. The grenade launcher is available in blue, purple and orange rarities, and is somewhat difficult to locate.

The Weapon Vault

In Fortnite there's a weapon vault where retired weapons rest in peace. The vault holds all sorts of different weapons, including the standard SMG as well as the crossbow. The vault is designed to help keep Fortnite balanced and also to encourage creativity. The developers of the game routinely retire weapons that aren't working out the way that they want them to. Serious players should keep updated on which weapons are still in the game and which ones are moving on. It's sad when your favorite weapon gets taken out of the game, but you can greet new and unique weapons as they come out, and before you know it you'll have a new favorite to make use of in the game.

SOME WEAPONS BREAK THE GAME

Some weapons are removed from Fortnite because they create a serious unbalance that forces players to search out and use one specific type of weapon in order to win. The

guided missile is one example of this type of weapon. With a massive amount of damage, and no real skill required to land attacks with this cannon it was a lethal tool that was being exploited by every player that could get his hands on it. There are few weapons that give players a serious advantage in combat, but the guided missile was one of them, which is exactly why it was removed from the game. The Zapotron

laser sniper rifle is another example of an overpowered weapon that was removed from the game. It was originally only available in supply drops, but was able to down players too easily and made the game very unbalanced.

BRINGING VAULTED WEAPONS BACK

If your favorite weapon gets removed from Fortnite, that's not necessarily a death sentence for it. It's called the Vault for a reason. Some weapons that are put into the vault are later added back into the game for players to use once again. In some instances the creators just need to take more time to figure out how to balance these weapons. In other instances, the creators just want to keep a certain weapon out for special events or to make room for another weapon that is eventually removed. Either way, it makes sense to keep an eye on vaulted weapons and regular updates because removed weapons can be added back in at any time.

The Vault is constantly changing, but staying up to date with it will help you learn what weapons to expect to find

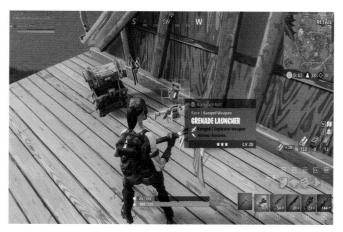

in your matches, and help you develop new strategies when your favorite tools are removed from Fortnite. You shouldn't spend all your time focusing on retired weapons, but it's smart to think about them a little and to stay up to date with Fortnite changes so you can figure out exactly how you're going to overcome your enemies.

Understanding Weapon Rarity

Every weapon in Fortnite comes in a special color that lets you know its rarity. There are five different rarity levels, and getting weapons from the low end and trading them up for high end weapons will help you do more damage and take out enemies more easily. As a serious Fortnite player, it's up to you to understand the different rarities and to make the most of them so that you are beating more enemies. That means trading in a green pistol for a blue one when you find it, and it means staying on the lookout for those rare drops that you won't find every time that you go into a house.

THE DIFFERENT RARITY LEVELS

There are five rarity levels for you to be aware of as you play Fortnite online. Once you learn which colors are the most valuable, you'll soon start seeing the good from the bad as you loot and you'll begin to build a better set of gear to fight with.

- Gray: Common
- Green: Uncommon
- Blue: Rare
- Purple: Epic
- Orange: Legendary

Gray weapons are all over the place and they are the weakest of all. These weapons deliver the lowest level of damage and they take longer to reload than all the other colors do of that same weapon type. Gray weapons are better than nothing at all, but you should be swapping in other colors for them as you find them. The one benefit of gray weapons is that you can find them just about anywhere, and you'll easily be able to find equipment to use if you are willing to use gray weapons.

Green weapons are a bit more difficult to find, but they are still laying all over the world and you should be able to find a green version of just about any weapon that you want to use in the game. These uncommon weapons are a bit more powerful, but should still be swapped out for blues and purples when you come across them. If you have a green you shouldn't have too much trouble downing other enemies with it, but don't count on defeating any person that you encounter with this tool.

Blue weapons or rare weapons are much more difficult to find. Many of the most popular weapons in the game come in this rarity and you should be able to locate them with a bit of searching. These weapons come out of chests more often than they are found in houses and other random spawn locations. If you want to build up your supply of rare weapons look for as many chests as you can while you play.

Purple or epic weapons are some of the most difficult to find in the game and include high powered tools like the SCAR assault rifle and a range of sniper rifles. Purple weapons come out of chests and loot drops and are tough to find on your own. If you like using this rarity level, your best bet is to take out enemy opponents and hope that they drop some high quality weapons as you remove them from the game.

Legendary weapons or the famed orange weapons are the most difficult to obtain and the most effective at killing enemies. They will deliver the maximum amount of damage for that specific weapon type, but legendary versions aren't always available for every weapon. It's possible to get a legendary bolt-action sniper, a legendary semi-automatic sniper, a legendary minigun, a legendary pistol and assault

rifle, but there are some tools that don't come in legendary. There is no legendary hunting rifle, or tactical or suppressed SMG or pump or tactical shotgun. If you're hoping to trade out those epic weapons for legendary ones make sure that you know which guns can be found in legendary rarity, and which ones simply aren't available in that form.

THE BENEFITS OF HIGHER RARITY

There are two major benefits that come along with having rarer weapons in Fortnite. Understanding the benefits will help you understand why it makes sense to search for those rare weapons and why you should be swapping out blues for greens, and golds for oranges. Always be on the lookout for better weapons and you'll improve your capabilities as the game goes on.

The first benefit is increased damage per round that you fire out of your weapon. Whether you are using pistols, shotguns, sniper rifles, rocket launchers or something else, going up from a Common to an Uncommon, or a Rare to an Epic will increase the amount of damage that you can deliver with your weapon with each and every shot that you fire off. That means that you can kill enemies faster and that you won't need as many rounds in order to defeat your opponents. This is more obvious with some weapons than others, but generally as you climb up to higher rarity levels you will be dealing more damage with your weapon.

The second benefit is on reload speed. Rarer weapons can be reloaded more quickly so that you can get back into the action that much faster. As an example the Revolver has a reload speed of 2.4 seconds when it's common or gray. When it's green or uncommon the speed drops to 2.3 seconds and when it's rare or blue the speed drops again down to 2.2 seconds. The change might not seem significant, but that split second advantage could be the only thing that allows you to dispatch an enemy before they can take you out.

Other than these common enhancements upgraded weapons don't offer too much of an advantage. Generally, all weapons of the same type have the same magazine size and firing rate. You won't have more bullets to make use of and you won't be able to fire them out any faster, but you will still do significantly more damage per second as you move from low quality weapons up to the higher quality options.

The Best Weapons for Victory

Everyone has different opinions about which weapons combination is best and which is worst in Fortnite, but there are certain item combinations that seem to work really well for most situations. We're going to cover several of the most common loadouts used by skilled players today and how to make the best of each of these weapon and consumable combinations. If you do decide to go with one of these combinations make sure that it matches your playstyle well and that you aren't just choosing a set of items that your favorite Fortnite player uses because you think they are cool or something.

A STANDARD LOADOUT

- **Assault Rifle**
- **Shotgun**
- **Sniper or Suppressed Pistol**
- **Explosive Weapon**
- **Medical Supplies**

This well-rounded loadout gives you plenty of damage output for both close and long-range fighting. At close range you should be using your shotgun to deliver as much damage as you can. At distance you can use your assault rifle or suppressed pistol to deliver damage and if you happen to have a sniper rifle this is an excellent tool to help you take out opponents at serious distance.

The recommended items for this loadout are the SCAR for your assault rifle, the heavy shotgun or pump shotgun, the bolt action sniper rifle, the best suppressed pistol that you can get, and rocket launchers for your explosive weapon. For your medical supplies you are best off with some form of shield, like a good stack of mini shield potions, but you will end up going with whatever items you happen to loot off of enemies and houses along the way to victory. This loadout is well-rounded and will give you the tools you need to crush many different types of enemies.

A DEFENSIVE LOADOUT

There are some Fortnite gamers that are constantly taking damage and just struggling to stay alive from one fight to the next, and these players will benefit from a more defensive loadout than the all-around loadout. In this loadout you are pretty much swapping your explosive weapons for additional healing capabilities, which will make some fights more difficult, but will help you stay alive more effectively over time. It's also important to stock up a high amount of materials if you're going to have a more defensive playstyle so you can constantly build defenses up to keep enemies off of you.

- Shotgun
- Assault Rifle
- Sniper Rifle
- Medical Supplies
- Medical Supplies

To make this loadout work you need to have the right playstyle to go with it. You should be a bit more defense minded during combat and try to stay alive more than you are trying to take out your enemies. For the shotgun that you go with you are best off with a heavy shotgun if you can find one, otherwise a pump or tactical will work fine. The SCAR is the preferred assault rifle to use, and you are free to pick up whatever sniper rifle you are most comfortable with. For your medical supplies you need to focus on supplies for shields and for life. That could mean mini shield potions and bandages. It could mean med kits and large shield potions. It could mean chug jugs and slurp juice. Just make sure that you have a combination of both shields and life healing tools and you'll be ready for any sort of damage.

THE SNIPER BUILD

Sniping is a whole lot of fun in Fortnite, but it's not as simple as it seems and there are certain item combinations that work best when you want to snipe all game long. That's why it's so important to take the time to learn which weapons and consumables you should be grabbing as you go around doing your early game looting.

- **Bolt action sniper or hunting rifle**
- **Sniper rifle**
- **Assault Rifle**
- **Shotgun**
- **Medical**

With this loadout your main strategy should be to land big shots on your enemies to either kill them instantly or knock them low enough that you can finish them off with your assault rifle. You want a bolt action rifle as your number one sniper, because this tool will allow you to one shot enemies

at range. For your second sniper you can go with whatever you like. The semi-automatic sniper works well in this slot because you get several shots to try and finish off weakened enemies and it's my favorite option for the second slot. After that you want an assault rifle for mid-range damage and a chance to finish off enemies hit by your sniper at mid-range distances. Finally you want the most powerful shotgun that you can get your hands on, preferably the heavy shotgun, and you want medical supplies for bandaging up, raising your shield and just keeping yourself from dying.

The sniper build is a lot of fun to play for anyone that enjoys sniping enemies, and it's something that you can use even before you are an expert sniper to help you develop your skills in the game.

THE STEALTH BUILD

When you want to take out enemies without them knowing where you are, the stealth build is a lot of fun to play around with and can actually be very effective. The trouble with this particular build is that it can be difficult to obtain all the different items that you need to make it work.

- **Silenced Pistol**
- **Silenced SMG**
- **Legendary Bush**
- **Shotgun**
- **Sniper Rifle**

This build is unique compared to the others because it doesn't include space for any sort of healing. When you rely on stealth the point is to avoid taking damage while eliminating your enemies, so you should be carefully engaging opponents and avoiding situations where you

need to heal as much as possible. With that said, if you want to enhance your survivability, you can swap out the sniper rifle or the silenced SMG for bandages, shields or other healing tools to help you avoid dying in combat.

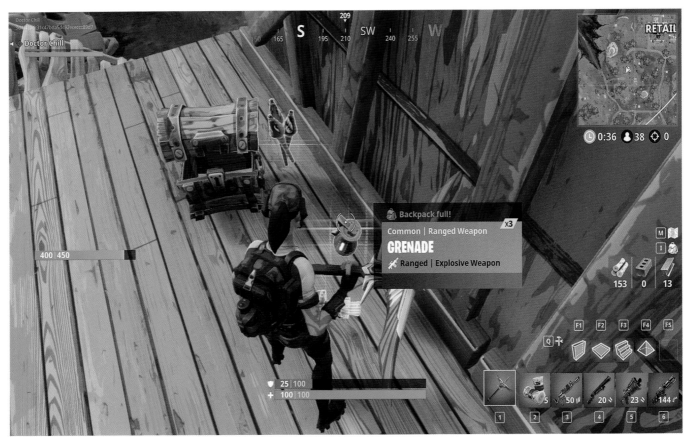

Utilizing Sticky and Standard Grenades

Grenades are one of the most underused weapons in Fortnite, even though they have the power to do a devastating amount of damage to the enemy. Not only that, but grenades are very easy to find when looting. For these reasons it makes sense to learn how to make the most of the different grenades so that you can deliver as much damage as possible to enemies. There are a few situations where the different grenade types are going to work best, and it's important to make the most of these situations to help yourself have some success in the game.

KILLING WITH STANDARD GRENADES

The basic grenades in Fortnite are some of the most difficult to get kills with, but can be extremely useful when used properly. There are a few situations where you'll want to use these grenades as often as you can. The first is when your enemy is down in a box fort or any other sort of base that has walls on most sides and doesn't have a roof, or has an exposed window. Just toss the grenade so it falls down inside the roof or goes through the window and there's a good chance you'll do explosive damage to the enemy.

Another way to use grenades is to take out enemies from around the corner. If you know that an enemy is approaching you from around a corner, you can toss the grenade so that it bounces around the corner and does damage to the approaching enemy.

For success with standard frag grenades don't make the mistake of trying to directly hit an enemy out in the open with them. Instead, rely on them when the enemy is in an enclosed space, and try to toss the grenade to go off as close to the enemy as possible while leading the enemy and thinking about their position. Just like with any other skill in the game, the more you toss out grenades the more likely you are to do damage with them.

KILLING WITH CLINGER GRENADES

Clinger grenades are a powerful weapon that can be used to one shot enemies with good enough accuracy. It's best to avoid using these grenades in direct conflicts when out in the open, but when used while peeking they can be very effective. The trick is to spot an enemy down below you, to peek out and toss a grenade that's going to stick directly to the target. This is easiest when the enemy isn't moving, but with enough practice you can lead the target and compensate for the grenade drop so that your toss sticks right to them. Over time as you throw enough clinger grenades you will be sticking more and more enemies and getting instant kills in the game. To help you learn the skill make sure you keep one slot with clinger grenades whenever possible and that you toss them out when you are in peeking situations. If you start going for grenade kills at close range before you attack with something like an assault rifle, you'll

get more one-shot kills and you'll avoid alerting the enemy of your position right away. This helps you survive longer and will result in more wins overall, so it's a good skill to try and learn as soon as you can.

Advanced Weapon Tactics

Beyond the basics like finding the rarest weapons possible, leading your enemies while sniping and working with the most effective weapons in different combat situations there are some other advanced attack skills that you should be aware of. These tactics will help improve your ability to overcome your enemies, and when making use of these skills you may even be able to get some kills with lower quality weapons compared to what your enemies are working with.

Peeking for Kills

Peeking is an essential skill in Fortnite and something that you should be using for most of your attacks. Instead of putting your entire body out in the open when you take a shot on your enemies, build up some defenses and peek out from behind them to take your shot. You'll take less damage from your enemies typically, and you'll be able to get more kills in your matches.

There are a few tips to make you more effective at peeking than the average player. The first is to wait a moment before moving out of cover to let your weapon crosshair shrink down to the highest level of accuracy. That way when you peek out and fire you'll be able to deliver your bullets to the desired target with absolute accuracy. If you rush to pop out and shoot you won't hit as many shots and won't get the kills that you want.

When peeking at your enemies you should also peek out at different locations from your cover. Peeking out from the same spot over and over again makes it simple for your enemies to land shots on you. By moving around your cover and peeking from different sections you take the enemy by surprise and make it easy to shoot them before they can shoot you.

Finally, when peeking try and pop out from the right side as much as possible. This is important to do because the Fortnite characters all hold weapons on the right side of their bodies. By peeking from the right side you can get your weapon out into the open to take a shot without exposing as much of your character. Peeking from the left side will put you out into the open more and make you easier to shoot for your enemies.

If you stick with each of these different strategies while peeking in Fortnite, you shouldn't have any trouble landing shots and avoiding damage effectively. That's why it's such a worthwhile tool for you to use, and why it's something that you should be adding into every single match that you are involved in as well.

Firing at Maximum Accuracy

With some weapons in Fortnite you need to fire as rapidly as possible to have a chance at beating your opponent. With others it's more important to wait until you are going to make the most accurate shots possible before you begin firing. For weapons like the burst assault rifle you should crouch down and wait a moment before firing off your first burst of rounds, because you'll reach a higher level of accuracy and enjoy improved killing potential by just waiting a moment. This is best accomplished by setting up cover like a ramp or a wall and then peeking out from behind it each time that you want to fire off a round. As you use a weapon you'll notice the crosshair circle growing smaller before you fire it. Firing the weapon will enlarge this crosshair, and so will moving around. If you take a moment to get the crosshair smaller, you'll enjoy more accurate shots and more effective kills as well.

Rocket Riding

Rocket riding is a fun strategy that's more for entertainment value than it is for actually getting kills or anything like that. It's a technique that involves two players on the same team, and essentially the one player jumps on and rides the rocket of another player. This can be used to quickly move across the map, to take shots at an enemy in a base high above you, or just to surprise other players in the game.

TAKING THE PERFECT SHOT

Successfully rocket riding is all about taking the perfect shot at the teammate that will be riding the rocket. To make this work you need to aim just above the waist of the other player and wait until the perfect moment. The player that's riding the rocket will jump into the air, and you must fire your rocket just as the other player reaches the highest point of their jump. Execute everything properly and the jumping player will land on top of the rocket and zip off away through the sky. This technique is a lot of fun, but it takes some time to master. That's why it's so important to really practice rocket riding before you try to do it for strategic purposes. With enough time you'll be executing rocket rides often and you might even get good at firing at other enemies while riding on top of a rocket across the map.

When you're in a serious battle with another player rocket riding isn't the best way to make use of your rocket launcher ammo. Instead you should be firing rockets to break apart

the enemy's base and open up kill shots for you and your teammates. If you're just interested in having fun or surprising the enemy, rocket riding can be an excellent way to do it. Give it a try with you and your friends and you'll have a bunch of great stories to tell about rocket riding in no time.

Careful Rocket Targeting

Rocket launchers are one of the most versatile weapon types in Fortnite, and also one of the most difficult tools to use effectively. In order to get as much as possible out of a rocket launcher you need to use it strategically. That means avoiding wasting rocket shots that are aimed at the wrong targets, and to start thinking about how your rocket launcher can give you a real edge over your enemies.

TARGET STRUCTURES FIRST

Rocket launchers are most useful for breaking through structures. The worst way to use rocket launchers is to try and kill enemies directly. Instead, aim at ramps, walls and other structures that you want to destroy. A rocket will tear right through an enemy structure, leaving them vulnerable to attack. The best way to use a rocket is to collapse ramps and get kills, but they work equally well to go through walls and other protective barriers. Look for weak spots in your opponent's defenses and fire off rockets right at those points. This will ensure that you are getting the most from the weapon and that you are making each and every rocket that you shoot off count.

AIM BEHIND THE ENEMY

The worst thing you can do with a rocket launcher is to try and hit an enemy directly. It's just too difficult to land a shot on your enemy since they will be running around so much. Instead, aim at a fixed point that's close to your enemy, or that you believe your enemy is running to. By targeting the fixed point you know where your rocket is going to land, and you have a good chance of delivering damage to your enemy with the splash damage from the explosion.

COMBINE ROCKETS WITH OTHER GUNS

Whenever you fire rockets at structures or your enemies fire off a round and then switch to a different gun to deliver more damage. If timed properly you can break through even tough walls with a mix of rockets and assault rifle fire so

that when the rocket hits the wall is eliminated and you are free to fire on the enemy. You can also fire straight through a demolished wall taken out by a rocket before the enemy has a chance to rebuild if you fire a rocket and start firing on the wall as the rocket is making impact. Don't just fire a rocket and wait to see how it does against the enemy, switch over to your other weapons and continue to deal damage as it makes its way to the target.

Rocket launchers are one of the most versatile weapons in all of Fortnite, but they won't do much for you if you aren't using them properly. They are a tool just like any other weapon in the game, and by following the tips above you can make the most of this tool to give yourself the tactical advantage every single time.

Collapsing Ramps

Ramps or staircases are one of the most heavily used structures in Fortnite, but they have a serious weakness that every player should be aware of. When the bottom of the staircase is destroyed, the whole structure will collapse. This is true for other structures as well, but because of how staircases work, they tend to be much easier to break down than others.

If you notice an enemy is climbing upward using a set of stairs or ramps, quickly destroy one of the lowest pieces to make the whole structure collapse. If the enemy is high enough up they will die on impact. If not, you can still take them out with your guns to finish the job that the ground started for you. Either way, taking out ramps is an effective strategy for picking off enemies.

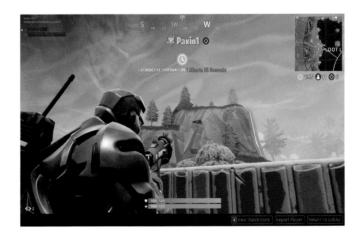

As you run around the world, keep an eye out for tall ramps that players may be lurking on. As a safety precaution take out any that you can along the way and you'll get some kills as a result as well.

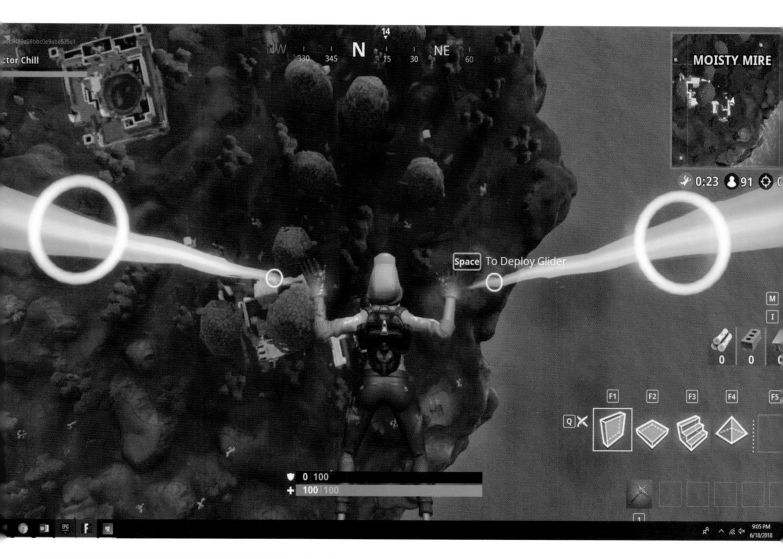

IMPULSE GRENADE LAUNCHING

Impulse grenades are a powerful tool that you can use to gain a positional edge over enemies that you face up against in Fortnite. These simple grenades aren't useful for doing damage on their own, but they can be a highly tactical tool that will help you do damage or make defensive moves that will keep you safe.

HOW THEY WORK

Impulse grenades put out a shockwave that will move anyone nearby dramatically. If you're standing on top of the grenade when it goes off you will be launched into the air. These grenades don't do any actual damage, but they can be used to do significant damage to your enemies or yourself if you aren't careful. That's why it's so important to understand different strategies that make the most of this unique tool.

LAUNCHING AN ENEMY

The number one way to use impulse grenades is to move your opponent around the field wherever you want them. If you have a spike trap laid down nearby to your opponent and you want them to get in range of it, toss out an impulse grenade and it can blast them over to the trap for serious damage. If there is an enemy standing on top of a ledge a quick impulse grenade might be all that it takes to knock that person over the side and make them fall down to their death. Impulse grenades will let you force an enemy to move in a specific direction, and with the right planning that move can result in the death of your enemy quite easily. Even if you don't want to use an impulse grenade to kill someone directly, you can use it to give yourself the edge in a fight as well. For instance, imagine that you are fighting someone with a shotgun and you have an assault rifle yourself. That person will want to get as close to you as possible during combat. Tossing an impulse grenade down in between the two of you will help create a large gap that you can use to help you land assault rifle shots while avoiding much of the damage from the shotgun. Impulse grenades are highly strategic, but with enough practice you should get used to them and maybe even find yourself making cool kills like those detailed above.

LAUNCHING YOURSELF

Impulse grenades aren't just a tool to use on your enemies though. Since it doesn't do any actual damage when launching the target away from it, it's possible to leverage these grenades to move your character around in ways that otherwise wouldn't be possible. To launch yourself up onto an enemy fort you could stand directly on top of the grenade which will send you flying into the air. Lay an impulse grenade down on the ground behind you to launch you toward an enemy so that you can get a kill with a shotgun or another close-range weapon. If you have a distance that you need to cover quickly, and you want to move around in an unpredictable manner, impulse grenades are the way to do it. These grenades are also really helpful for getting out of the storm and into safety as soon as possible. If you are in a hurry these grenades can help you cross the distance that you have to cover as fast as you possibly can.

If you've never used impulse grenades before, or if you skipped over them because they seemed difficult or useless, pick them up the next time you see them and give them a try. While they do take some time to get the hang of using, these potent grenades are powerful strategic tools that will help you move your character and enemy characters around in combat. The grenades are pretty simple to use and allow you to overcome opponents in a bunch of different ways that might not work out for you otherwise.

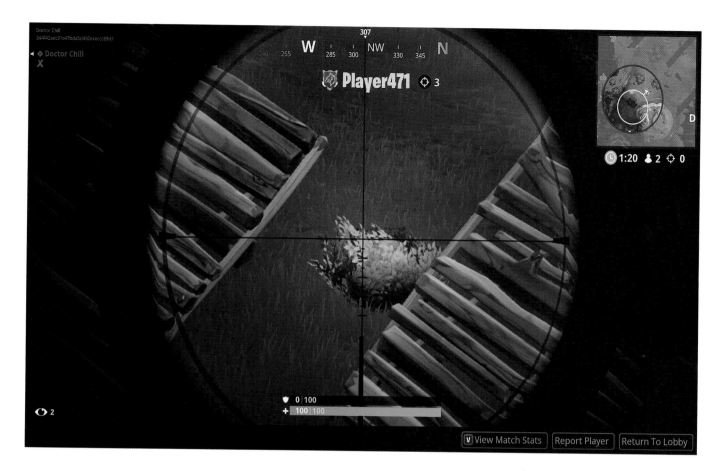

Effective Sniping

Sniper rifles are arguably the most important of all the weapons in Fortnite. They allow you to take out enemies before they are even able to see you, and with the right strategy you can gain a serious tactical edge in battle with a sniper rifle.

ACCOUNTING FOR BULLET DROP

Unlike most of the other guns in Fortnite, the sniper rifle suffers from bullet drop. That means that as you shoot over a long enough distance, the bullets will fall down to a lower location than where you originally started from. If you're shooting at an enemy from a long distance with the sniper, you will actually have to aim higher than where you want to hit them. Raising your crosshairs up a bit will help make sure that when your bullet drops down it will land right on the enemy that you are aiming at. If you raise the crosshairs

too high you'll miss your shot, and if you move them too low you'll miss that powerful headshot that will almost always take your enemy out of the game.

It can be difficult estimating the right amount of bullet drop to account for, especially when you're just getting started in the game. However, you can fix this issue by just taking the time to learn how to snipe properly and you'll get a whole lot more kills in battle by knowing the skill. The best way to figure out what sort of bullet drop you're dealing with is to just practice sniping as much as possible. That means, once you are fortunate enough to find a sniper rifle and some ammo, get into a tower and start firing off as many shots as you can on the enemy. You'll miss many of your shots, but over time you will start to land more and more of them. Usually bullet drop is smaller than you think as a new player, so don't aim way over top of the enemy when trying to land a shot. Instead, fire off a round that's just above the enemies head and that only leads the enemy slightly, this is the best way to start firing and will lead to the most accurate shots.

Landing shots initially is so difficult because bullet drop adjustments change depending on the distance, and whether the enemy is above or below you when you are firing

at them. Instead of trying to think about all these different variables when you are taking shots, it's best to just focus on practicing shot after shot and eventually you'll pick up the skills and start landing your snipes. Just keep these different factors in mind when you are learning how to land sniper shots and eventually you'll get the hang of this difficult skill.

CHOOSING A SNIPER TO USE

There are two different sniper rifles that are worth consideration when you have the option, the bolt action and the semi-automatic sniper. Most highly skilled players prefer the bolt action sniper because it delivers the maximum damage per round. Less skilled players often prefer the semi-automatic sniper though, because they can readjust after their first shot and keep firing to become more accurate. When learning to snipe the semi-automatic rifle is your friend. After you get very good, you'll want to swap to the bolt-action whenever possible for more effective killing.

COVERTLY SNIPING

Sniping works so well on enemies for a few different reasons. Number one is because you are firing from such a long distance that many of your enemies simply won't be able to fire back accurately and do much damage to you. The second reason is because you should be quite difficult to spot. It's up to you to make sure you are well hidden before you start firing off sniper rounds. This is especially true if there is another sniper nearby. To do this, you should be positioning yourself in a tower or some other hidden location where you are barely visible. You should peek out just before taking a shot, adjust your aim, fire and then hide once again. By following this technique you will limit how long you are out in the open, reducing the chances that the enemy will spot you and hit you with a good shot.

Sniping is one of the most useful skills to develop in Fortnite, and one of the most difficult. It's not something that you'll master immediately, but once you do get it down you'll get many more kills than you used to. Just make sure you are thinking about bullet drop and leading your enemies, and that you are taking plenty of practice shots with any sort of sniper that you can find. Over time the skill will come. ★

The Advanced Building Guide

IN FORTNITE, BUILDING IS LIFE. If you don't know how to build, you're going to put yourself at a serious disadvantage every single time that you come face to face with an enemy. Building can help you accomplish any goal that you have in the game and it's one of the keys to winning matches. Understanding how to build quickly and effectively will allow you to take the higher ground in any matchup. It will let you block incoming fire and keep your character alive for much longer. A good building can give you the edge you need to beat out an unsuspecting group of enemies, even when you're on your own. Learn to build well, and you'll find that the rest of Fortnite becomes much easier. You don't need to be an expert marksman to do well in Fortnite, but you absolutely need to be able to build well.

If you aren't confident with building just yet, don't worry, developing this advanced skill takes time. The best way to start is to use some basic building techniques and to work up to the more advanced stuff later on. In this section we'll cover basic building information like which materials are best for different situations, but we'll also go into advanced building techniques, different building structures and how to edit your buildings to make them even more effective. Pay close attention and you'll know all that you need to know to become a pro builder in this highly popular shooter!

Understanding Starting and Finished HP for Materials

There are three different materials that you have to work with when putting up any sort of building: wood, brick and metal. Each of these materials has different properties that you should be aware of, and only one material is going to be the best option depending on the situation that you're in. Learn which material is best for each situation and you'll know just what to use when you get into trouble.

USE WOOD FOR SPEED

Wood is the strongest material when you need initial strength more than anything else. That's because a wooden wall starts out at 100 HP and grows in strength faster than brick or metal does until it reaches 200 HP. If you're looking to keep bullets away from your body and the shooter is right in front of you, go with wood every single time. It will hold up better and provide you the protection that you need to reach cover. Wood gains life much faster than brick or metal when it's being built, and that makes it the most effective option until after it hits its peak at 200 HP, which takes about 6 seconds.

USE METAL FOR STRENGTH

When long-term strength is the most important value that you're interested in, metal is the way to go. This resource becomes tougher over time and is the most durable material when it's been set in position for about 7 seconds. That means, if you have more than 7 seconds before you're going to be attacked, metal is almost always the best tool for building your base. Metal walls offer 400 HP when they are completely constructed, and will hold up to some serious damage while other materials would quickly fail. Sniper towers and other common long-term structures are crafted from metal, but the most important section of a building to make out of metal is the area that will house actual people. Make sure that when you use metal for building you use it in any location where you will be taking fire regularly, and then fill in with the lower quality materials in other locations as needed.

USE BRICK AS A SUBSTITUTE

Brick isn't the best material for anything, but that doesn't mean that you should throw away any brick that you happen to pick up. Brick offers less protection than wood when you first lay it down, and it offers less protection than metal when it's fully built. It's an interesting material because it's pretty boring and rarely the best option, but brick can play an important role in your matches as well, as a substitute. When you would like to lay wood down for protection, brick is the next best option if you run out of wood. When you would prefer laying metal down for long term durability, brick should be used instead of wood. Make use of brick when you don't have the optimal material for the job, and you'll still enjoy better results than if you used metal in place of wood or the other way around.

How Many Materials Are Enough?

At the beginning of each match of Fortnite you have to think a bit about how many materials you want to get so you know when you can stop gathering and start focusing on building up your loot supply. For most standard players a few hundred wood with some brick and metal thrown in is all that you need. You can quickly build this supply up from trees and pallets and you'll be on your way to building effective structures throughout your match. Even though you're going to use far more than 200 wood during a match, you will probably be okay with that amount when you get started because you're going to loot more materials off the players that you take out throughout the match. If you last long enough to burn through all your wood, you should get at least a few kills during that process and reload your materials so you're ready for more fights in the future.

THE BEST LOCATIONS FOR FINDING MATERIALS FAST

If you know that you're going to build a massive structure, or you just want to be able to stock up your materials quickly, there are a few locations on the Fortnite map that are best to drop down on to load up on materials very rapidly. Two locations jump out above all the rest when you value resources, Moisty Mire and Wailing Woods. Both of these options are ideal because they are jam packed with large trees that you can break down quickly. Some of the trees will give you 117 wood when you break them, and it only takes a few seconds to chop them down when hitting the critical strike locations.

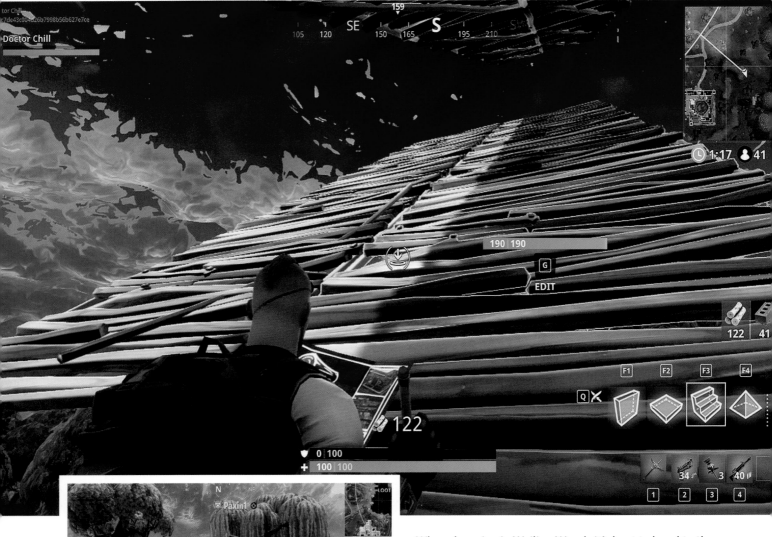

When dropping in Wailing Woods it's best to head to the center of the maze if it's not overrun by other players. There's a chest in the house at the middle of the maze, and two additional chests throughout the maze for you to gear up from. After a quick gear up you can head out into the large trees and build up your materials stockpile rapidly.

If you don't like either of those two locations, you can also drop near the large structures at Loot Lake and build up a supply of materials rapidly from the buildings there, but it's not as efficient as the Wailing Woods or Moisty Mire is and you'll spend a bit more time stockpiling materials before you have enough to comfortably move on.

When dropping down in Moisty Mire one of the best starting locations is just above the lettering for Moisty Mire on a small island in between surrounding water. There's a large tree in this location that spawns two chests and also serves as a useful resource for building up your material stockpile.

Protecting Ramps and Making Wider Ramps

Ramps are one of the most important tools that you have at your disposal in Fortnite, but they are also one of the weakest of all the structures. Ramps will allow you to get up into a desirable position quickly so that you can shoot down at your enemies without them being able to shoot you very well. Even though ramps are so effective and a must-use building block, they also put you at risk when you climb up on them. That's because ramps all collapse when broken. If you have 10 ramps all going up and you're standing at the top, an enemy only needs to take out the bottom ramp to send you hurtling down to your death. That's why it's

so important to take extra precautions to protect yourself when you use ramps. There are a few different ways that you can do that that we'll touch on.

WALLING YOUR RAMPS

One of the simplest ways to protect ramps that you build is throwing walls around them. This is common when building small bases, but it can also be used when creating raised structures. Wall up any portion of ramp that you believe is going to be attacked and you won't have to worry about your structure collapsing as easily. Adding a wall here forces the player to work harder to break your building, and it means that you have time to react and possibly take them out before they can do any real damage to you.

USING DOUBLE RAMPS

Another very effective strategy to avoid the ramp collapse problem is to double up the ramps that you build. If you create two ramps as you build upwards the enemy will have to shoot through both ramps before your structure collapses. This buys you additional time as well and can be the difference between living and dying for many players. If you're going to build a large structure that relies heavily on ramps, and you plan on staying there for an extended time, make sure that you use two ramps side-by-side. Sure you'll go through many more materials building in this way, but you'll be safer and have a more effective structure thanks to your hard work.

Editing Your Builds

It's possible to build plenty of simple structures with the building blocks as they come out as standard, but things get much more interesting when you start editing your structures. Each of the different basic building blocks can be altered in a number of special ways through the editing tool. Fortnite makes it possible to very quickly change the way that a piece looks and functions just by opening up the editor and making adjustments.

To open the editor face the object you wish to edit and press "G" when playing on PC, hold "Circle" on PlayStation or hold "B" on Xbox. Once you do this a series of blue squares will appear, and you can adjust the final look and function of the object by turning the squares on or off depending on what you want to accomplish. Each object has a wide variety of edited forms, and it's possible to create a wide range of final shapes with editing.

Actively Editing Your Structures

Editing is one of the most useful techniques in Fortnite building because it allows you to make your buildings much more fluid. Imagine for a second a player that doesn't know how to edit. They are getting attacked and quickly wall themselves in to start healing and avoid taking damage. This is a good strategy, but they are trapped within that box after healing because they don't know how to edit. As a skilled player that can edit effectively, that player can throw in doors, adjust walls to be triangles and seamlessly move through their structure to get away or move to a different

section of it and overcome an enemy. In Fortnite, structures can be edited repeatedly, and you can very quickly switch from full to half walls to take shots and then close yourself back in again once you get the hang of editing properly.

By learning to actively edit objects you'll be a more effective builder and create new opportunities for you to kill your enemies before they can take a shot at you. You'll start surprising enemies and moving around in ways that they don't expect you to, which is key in a game as competitive as Fortnite. That's why you need to take the time to learn all the different object edits you can make in Fortnite, and then practice making those edits quickly so that you can take full advantage of them during combat.

Use the Same Edits Again and Again

There are some edited materials that you'll want to reuse repeatedly while in Fortnite and that's alright. If you want to lay down 30 spiral staircases, you don't need to edit a ramp every single time that you put one down. Instead, you can use the game's edit save feature to keep laying down the same thing over and over again. To make this happen, you simply press the edit button and select the building block that you want to lay down and make all the necessary changes to create the edited object that you want. Once you do this you'll lay down your first edited object, and you can continue to keep using the edited object again and again. To use it just lay down the object while holding the edit button down again. The game holds the last edit and will make the same changes again and again as you play.

CREATING UP AND DOWN RAMPS

One way to make the most of saved edits is to make an up ramp and a down ramp. For the up ramp you just use the basic ramp or staircase object and lay it in front of you. For the down ramp you edit a roof into a downward facing ramp. Now, you can very quickly switch from the ramp to the roof object to create up and down ramps as needed. You can switch directions very rapidly using this technique and can move vertically as necessary without having to rotate your ramps around at all.

Building custom structures that rely heavily on different edited objects isn't difficult to do when you make use of the edit save function of Fortnite. If you've never tried editing an object before laying it down, give it a try to see how the game will save your edit for future use, and you'll quickly start coming up with ways to gain the edge over your enemies while in heated combat.

Walls

Walls are by far the most versatile of all the building materials and they offer an excellent level of protection when used properly. Standard walls will keep enemies away from you, but edited walls can give you a view of the enemy while also offering you protection. We've outlined all the different edited wall options and how you can make the most of these items.

ADDING DOORS

You can add doors in three different positions on a wall by removing two squares vertically stacked from the bottom up. Take out two squares on the left to put a door there. Remove them from the center to add a door there and remove them from the right side to add a door there.

SHORT WALL

When you want to create a wall that's low enough to jump and shoot from, simply remove all the top squares from the wall in editing. This will shorten the wall down enough to still provide you with full cover while standing up, but allow you to jump up and take a shot if you want to. This is effective when you want to surprise enemies, or make it difficult for them to hit you while you are firing on them.

MICRO WALL

If you take out the top two rows of blocks when editing a wall you'll end up with a tiny wall that's high enough to protect you when crouching. Put this wall into position when you want to be able to crouch for cover and pop up to take shots or angle up from the wall to opponents slightly higher than you are.

DOORED SHORT WALL

For a wall that you can jump up over to shoot at your opponent, that also offers an easy exit location, you can create a doored wall. To do this, remove the entire top row of squares, then remove the squares that you would normally remove for a door. This creates a short wall with a full-sized door in it. You won't be able to shoot over the door well, but can shoot over the other sections easily with a quick hop.

ARCHWAY

For a massive archway that takes up the entire wall in width, you must remove the entire bottom row of the wall and the center block of the next row up, leaving behind a small blue archway above you. It's good for creating plenty of open space, but generally dangerous when used on bases and other protective structures.

ANGLED WALL

To transform your wall into a triangle that's approximately half the wall in size you need to take out three blocks in a corner. Take out the lower right block, the block above it and to the left of it and you'll make a triangle wall that starts to the left and goes up to the right. You can make four different triangles depending on which of the corners you remove so play around with this to create some pretty unique structures.

ADDING A WINDOW

Finally, you can add a window to your wall to create points to look out and shoot from. To add a window you simply remove the block in the middle row of wall. A block on the side of the central row of blocks will create a small window with a short wall piece for the case. Removing the block right at the very center of the wall will create a larger window that's centered perfectly. Windows are a key component in many bases and they create a convenient vantage point to shoot and snipe from while you play.

Platforms

Platforms are much more versatile than most Fortnite players realize. Sure they're good for ledges and for creating bridges from one location to another, but they also provide protective coverage against flying explosives above you, and they can be used to create some pretty cool structures as well.

CREATE A CORNER WALL

Remove a single block from your platform to create a short raised wall that points in two different directions. This gives you a small amount of cover from enemies when you crouch down behind it and it's simple to create.

CREATE A FULL WALL

Delete two blocks in a row and you'll create a short wall
in that space for you to crouch behind. This is particularly
useful when editing the top of a tower or another building
where you want just a bit more protection. When you're
fighting down on the ground you can use this technique to
give you slightly more cover, though you won't have much of
an advantage over enemies that are above you.

CREATE A CURVED WALL

When it's just you against enemies from multiple sides, one
of the best forms of cover that you can create for yourself is
the curved wall. Delete all but a single square where you're
going to stand and the other squares will transform into
a mini wall. Delete the squares in all the directions of your

enemies and you'll have a nice curved wall to crouch behind
while you gun them down.

RAMPS

Ramps are arguably the most useful structure in Fortnite and one of the most heavily used as well. Without ramps you can't get up above your enemy. While most people rely on basic ramps when in heated combat, there are actually advanced versions of this very simple structure that offer new capabilities you might not have considered. Learn more about the edited variations of stairs and you'll quickly start thinking of added possibilities.

EDITING RAMPS IS UNIQUE

Once you begin editing ramps you'll quickly notice that they are unique compared to the other objects in the game. That's because there is a directional arrow on the editor as well as a block selector. By selecting which blocks are involved and the direction the ramp must follow, you create a unique layout that determines what the ramp is like once laid down.

HALF RAMP WALL

To create a half ramp that has a protective wall, drag the blocks straight in front of you so half of them turn blue and there is an arrow facing away from you. This creates a half ramp and puts a wall up in the location of the other set of blocks.

THE TURNING RAMP

It's also possible to create a turning ramp setup that actually acts like a staircase that might be in your home. Start the structure with a horizontal arrow from one block to the other. This is the direction that the first flight of stairs heads in. From there drag from the second block up to the third. If you finish the structure here you'll end up with a ramp structure that ends in the direction of that next block. You can also drag the ramp in a "U" shape

going horizontally, then vertically and horizontally to the final ramp, which creates a longer landing and faces the final ramp in the horizontal direction opposite to the direction of the initial ramp.

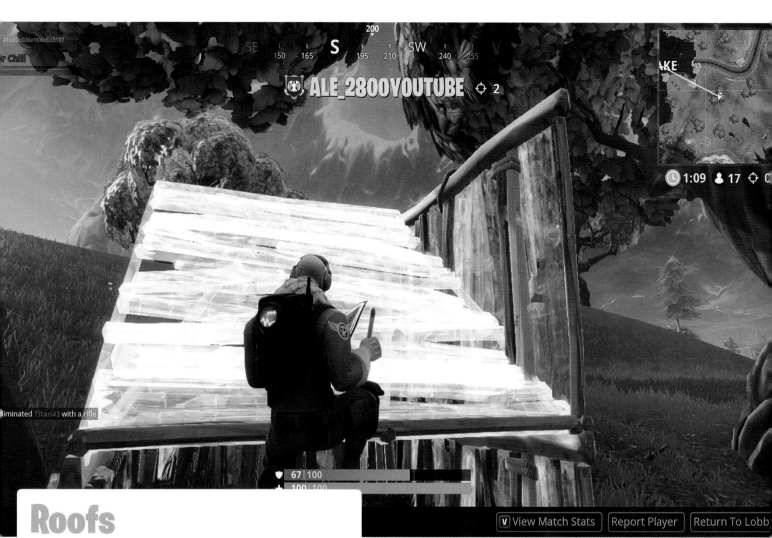

Roofs

Defensively, roofs or the pyramid shaped building blocks are one of the most useful tools that you'll encounter in Fortnite once you learn how to use them properly. Even just dropping a single pyramid onto the ground gives you head-height cover and allows you to quickly climb up and target your enemies. Pyramids also make excellent roofs and can be added to a wide range of structures, but they become infinitely more interesting as you begin to edit them.

THE HALF TEEPEE

Remove one of the two corners closest to you while in the editor and you'll create what looks like a cutout from a teepee. You get two tall sloped walls and a hollow section that you can walk down under for excellent cover. The best part of this structure is that you can climb the sloped walls and easily target your enemies from up above while walking back slightly to give yourself cover.

THE PYRAMID RAMP

To quickly swap a pyramid into a ramp structure, just edit out all the squares except two squares running in the same direction. You'll get a ramp that looks very similar to a standard Fortnite ramp with the wood running vertically instead of horizontally.

THE PROTECTIVE VALLEY

To create a raised valley with two angled walls to come up from it, leave just only one of the bottom corner squares and remove all the rest. The valley will show up in the direction of the square opposite of the remaining square.

Editing for Vision

All those advanced edited structures are good for helping to create exactly the building you're looking for and also to adapt buildings as needed during combat, but that's not all the editor is good for. When you're protected by your own structures, you can also use the edit menu to see your enemies through solid objects. Imagine that you are protected with walls on every single side of you. You obviously can't see where your enemies are on the other side of those walls, and if you create a window in the wall to see you'll be opening yourself up to attack. With a bit of help from the editor you can remedy this issue without exposing yourself to attack.

Instead of changing the form of the object you want to see through, just open the editor up and look through the object then close the editor once again. Objects become see-through when the editor is turned on, and with that menu open you can very easily see around you past that

object that's blocking your enemy's view. The next time that you're deciding what you should do and trying to guess where your enemy is on the other side of your base, just edit look through a wall and pinpoint exactly where the enemy is. You'll be able to make more reliable decisions and maybe even kill your enemy as a result. Just make sure that you don't keep the editor open too long or you could be left defenseless when the enemy comes crashing through the side of your base!

Utilizing Traps

There are three different traps in Fortnite, each one has an effective use that will help give you an edge over your enemies. There are spike traps meant for inflicting damage to enemies, campfires meant to heal you and your allies up and launch pads meant to give you a mobility advantage to get above your enemies or to escape quickly.

LAYING TRAPS

Traps are simple to lay down and work just like any other building material. While on PC just press "F5" to switch to your trap and lay it down into position. You can only hold one trap type at a time, so make sure that you have the one you want most in your inventory.

When on PlayStation or Xbox you need to switch to builder mode and tab over to your trap to lay it down. To do that you need to press "B" on Xbox and "Circle" on PlayStation. Once in builder mode you simply tab over to the trap and then lay it down. On Xbox that means pressing "RB" to tab over and "RT" to lay the trap down. On PlayStation that means pressing "L1" and then "L2" and finally "R2" to put the trap into position.

USING SPIKE TRAPS EFFECTIVELY

Spike traps can be placed on walls, roofs and floors and they are highly visible traps that deliver an excellent amount of damage. Spike traps have recently been set to 150 damage, which makes them lethal enough to take out enemies as long as they don't have a full shield and full health. Even if they do have those things, a well-placed trap will soften them up, so you can get the easy kill yourself.

To use spike traps well, carefully position them so that the enemy is less likely to notice them while walking through a room. Put them on the ceiling or a wall instead of the floor. If you are a very fast builder you can also trap your enemy in a box and put traps around them for a fun and challenging kill, though this is the least practical way to utilize spike traps.

Spike traps are a fun tool for getting kills and work even better when you bait them. Leave these powerful traps next to chests or with powerful items sitting down below them and enjoy the thrill of bringing in kill after kill from enemies that try to pick up the loot.

LAYING TRAPS IN REAL TIME

An advanced way to use traps in Fortnite is to actually lay them as players are entering a room that you're in. This only works if you can lay the traps extremely quickly which means practicing regularly. It makes sense to lay traps as a person is coming into the room with you because most skilled players won't enter a room if they hear you set a trap. If you set the trap as they are already entering they won't stop what they are doing and you're almost guaranteed to hit them with the trap while you use a shotgun to finish them off. Since traps were recently enhanced this technique is lethally effective even with a single trap, and it's something that you'll want to start doing to catch players off guard as you fight them.

MAKING THE MOST OF CAMPFIRES

Campfires are technically traps, though they won't be doing damage to anyone. These little traps can be laid on the ground and they heal all your nearby allies. That means when you are in a full squad you can easily raise the health of everyone by laying down a campfire. This tool raises health by a total of 50 HP per person, and they can be a simple way to restore your life after you take damage, though it does take time to get back to full health using a campfire.

Toss a campfire down in the center of your base to bring your characters back to full health, or toss one down while healing up behind a wall to speed up your life recovery further.

MAKING THE MOST OF LAUNCH PADS

Launch pads are like overpowered trampolines that dramatically enhance mobility on Fortnite for a short period of time. They can be used in a few different ways. Toss down a launch pad to quickly climb up onto an enemy's fort or to get up onto a nearby hill. Also lay down a launchpad and use it to escape from your own base when it's invaded by the enemy. If you need to move through the air quickly, a launch pad can help you do just that.

By taking the time to practice with different traps, you can give yourself an edge in different situations and stop throwing away those traps in favor of other simpler objects.

Base Designs

Now that you have a general idea of how to build and to edit the blocks that you place down, it's time to focus on creating advanced base structures. With enough practice making some of these structures, you'll be able to create them quickly and easily. Before you know it, you'll be building around your enemies and overwhelming them with your skills before they even know how to respond.

A Single Ramp Box

This is one of the simplest defensive structures and something that you'll use constantly while battling in Fortnite. To make this structure add four walls around your character, stand in the center of the walls, jump up and toss a ramp down below your feet. That's all there is to it. The walls protect your ramp from being destroyed, and the ramp allows you to climb up and pick off your opponents to the front or side of you.

You can modify this basic structure in a few different ways to make it even more useful. One way is to add additional walls to the sides of your simple base at the top for some side protection, or to wall off the back of the base for protection

behind you in case someone comes up from another angle. You should also consider adding a door to the back of your base at the bottom of the ramp by editing the wall. As long as no enemies are behind you, you can easily escape out the door if you have enemies breaking in from the front, or sneaking around the side of your base.

While in the single ramp box it's important to keep a platform ready so that you can roof off your space if an enemy tosses a grenade at you. If you are quick enough you can block the grenade and keep yourself safe and ready to continue fighting once again. Without a platform or roof, a grenade can very easily kill you inside this base type.

Another cool variation on the single ramp box is to add an outward ramp from each of the side walls of your base, creating a sort of funnel for you to climb around on. This funnel structure has four exposed ramps that are easy to destroy, but it gives you additional points of cover and makes it easier to pick off enemies that are close to your base.

Double Ramp Box

The double ramp box is a simple variation on the single ramp box and ideal for playing in Duos or even some squad matches. To build this structure place two walls between you and your enemy side-by-side. Then add side walls and back walls to create a rectangular base. Now jump and lay down two ramps side-by-side, giving you and your teammate a defended location to fight the enemy from. Once in position you can easily add on doors, additional walls up above and make other modifications to your structure. You can make it an even more durable and effective base, but this basic structure is good enough to beat most typical ground-based enemies.

Funnel Base

A funnel base is an interesting variation of the standard ramp base we mentioned earlier, and it creates a more diverse structure that makes it easy to pick off enemies from all around you. To create this simple base you need to make two ramps facing opposite directions from one another to form a "V" shape. Now wall around these ramps entirely to give yourself a blocked off trench to climb in and out of while fighting off the enemies. This structure is quick and easy to make and creates enough space for two players to defend against incoming enemies.

To enhance this structure further it's possible to use double or triple ramps all laid in a row to create a longer "V" formation

so more people can move about comfortably when fighting. Just be sure to add walls around all of it for necessary protection when fighting. By making the "V" formation longer, you can also cover some of the funnel with platforms to create a small roofed off area to duck into when being fired on by grenades so that you can heal up safely.

Sniper Tower

The sniper tower is one of the simplest and most effective structures for getting above the other players on the map and making a good point for sniping enemies, creating a powerful sky base or preparing for high level combat later in the game.

THE BASIC STRUCTURE

To start off your sniper tower you need to build four walls enclosing your character. Now stand to one side of the box and put a ramp in the center of it. This is the basic structure of your tower and you'll essentially just repeat the process to go up in the air and give yourself the perfect height to take on your enemies.

BUILDING THE TOWER

To effectively build the sniper tower you make the four walls and single ramp, then you climb up the ramp to the highest position and add four additional walls on top of the first four. From there you jump and lay a ramp down over the initial ramp. Now you climb up that new ramp, add four more walls jump and lay your next ramp. Continue this process until you are high enough off the ground that you are ready to start sniping the enemy. Once you are in position you can add some platforms to make a nice floor, toss in some walls with windows, add a roof over top of it and start picking off the enemy. It's as simple as that and you can climb really high vertically without using too many materials in the process.

ESCAPING FROM THE TOWER

If you're taking serious damage or your tower is being ripped down it's important that you can escape so you don't die inside. To do this effectively you need to have plenty of resources remaining. To get out of your base you just knock one of the four walls down up top, select a ramp and rotate it around so its going down and away from you. Now build a long ramp from you down to the ground or as close to the ground as you can get. Quickly escape from your tower using your ramp and go find a new spot to hide and heal up before you engage the enemy once again.

Sky Base

Building a sky base is very similar to creating a sniper tower. You can form a sky base by building a sniper tower and then building platforms off from it from there. Some players build multiple sniper towers up to a sky base to make it more durable and difficult to break down. Once you have the sniper tower up to the height that you want, just build outward with platforms from there. Get enough platforms to make a nice stable base, and then start building up little towers, walls and other locations for you to hide and shoot from.

When building a sky base to try and win the match from, make sure to construct it at the center of the storm eye, so that you have the best chance of remaining in the safe zone as borders are adjusted. It's also possible to expand your sky base outward to remain inside the eye of the storm if some of your sky base slips outside the safe zone, but you'll need a huge amount of resources to be able to accomplish this feat.

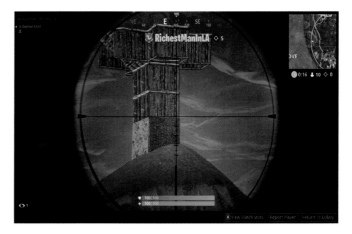

There are so many different variations on the standard base design that you can always create something unique or enhance a base with additional resources and adustments as needed. The key to building effectively in Fortnite is to get comfortable using each of the four building blocks, and then laying them down as needed in the middle of combat and while creating more advanced structures in the game.

Making the Most of Turbo Mode

Thanks to recent changes within Fortnite, building fast is easier than ever before. The developers of the game added something known as Turbo Mode. Turbo Mode makes it easier for new players to build faster and more effectively. Players can now hold down the build button and automatically lay down ramps, walls, platforms or roofs by just dragging their view in different directions. This might not seem like a significant enhancement, but it's a powerful tool that every new player should be using to help speed up their building.

To make use of Turbo Mode, hold down the build button and then move your view around in the direction that you want to build. To quickly build ramps you just need to hold build on the ramp button and run upward and ramps will appear

before you. To effectively build a double ramp you just need to swing your view from side to side as you run upwards.

You can also make use of Turbo Mode to quickly wall yourself in on all sides. To do this, hold the build button on the wall and spin around in a circle rapidly. You'll toss walls down all around you and you can easily build a few layers of walls in a square around you using this technique.

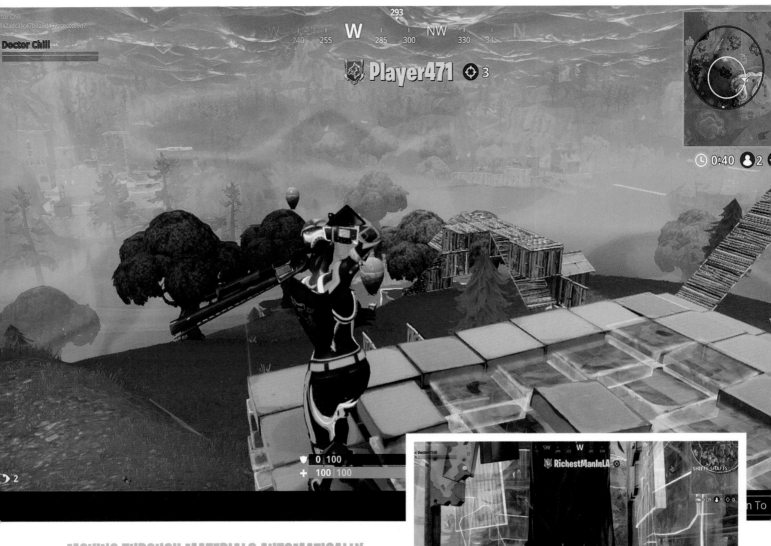

MOVING THROUGH MATERIALS AUTOMATICALLY

New enhancements in Fortnite now make it possible to seamlessly move from one material to another as you run low while building. That means that if you start building with wood you'll move through brick and metal as you run out of each material. By just building without worrying about changing material types manually, you can lay structures down faster and become more effective at overwhelming our enemies. This is a feature that many players don't realize is in the game, and it's something that you should be using whenever you can.

By utilizing Turbo Building mode and the game's auto material switching features you can easily build faster and more effectively when it matters most. If you're going too slowly while in combat you're going to lose. If you build rapidly enough you'll come out on top in conflict almost every time.

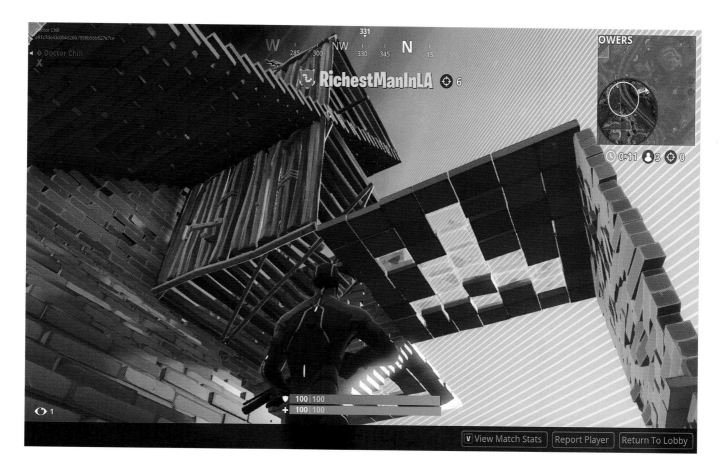

Combat Building

As a newer player in Fortnite much of the building that you'll be doing is for the purpose of protecting your character and keeping damage from ever reaching you. That's not the only reason that you want to be able to build well though. Expert players also use building as an offensive tool to actually do damage and overcome enemies. Combat building is a technique meant to maximize the damage you can do, and to also give yourself rapid defense as needed while you are in the middle of a fight. It's not the same as casually laying down a base or a sniper tower to attack enemies from later on, it's a reactive kind of building that you'll have to learn over time. Below are some helpful combat building tips and techniques to help you overcome opponents with your building speed, efficiency and creativity, and with enough practice you'll be overwhelming opponents before you know it.

TRAPPING AND EDITING

While in heated combat with your enemy, it's vital that you trap them as much as you possibly can as you are building up. That means laying platforms over top of their buildings. It means creating stairways and platforms up above them, and it means walling them in. If you can effectively box in your opponent, you have a free kill with some simple strategic play. Once your enemy is locked into position, you only need to edit through the walls, ramps and platforms that you have laid down to create an opening that you can attack through. Since your enemy has no way of knowing what piece you'll be editing, they won't see the attack coming, giving you a huge tactical advantage.

The trick to making this strategy work is being able to edit structures quickly, and being able to build faster and with more strategic success than your enemy. If you can build around the enemy before they can get up and above you, you have essentially already defeated them.

If you lay down enough blocks around your enemy, you can still overcome them even if you run out of materials first. That's because you'll have the power to edit all your pieces and move around freely, while they are more limited. You can weave in and out of your creations and attack the enemy from an unexpected angle.

THE FASTEST WAY TO GAIN THE HIGH GROUND

While in combat gaining the high ground is the most important goal that you should have in mind at all times. For that reason, it makes sense to focus on a technique that's as fast as possible. Many players rely on turbo building walls around them and then placing a ramp over and over again to climb vertically rapidly, but there is an even faster technique available. Instead of using walls and ramps, use platforms and ramps. Lay down a ramp and then jump and place a platform and jump and place

a ramp and switch back and forth between the two. With expert building skill it's possible to go up four stories in just three seconds using this technique, and you can move upward much faster than an opponent can if they are using a different technique to climb. This even works better than just laying out straight ramps and running upward.

The only issue with climbing in this way is that it's very easy to collapse this structure. That's why it's important to avoid climbing too high with this technique, and to focus on growing above your opponent and then using platforms to block their progress upward so you can start laying the damage down and going for the kill. Avoid using this technique when building long-term structures, and just rely on it for gaining high ground rapidly and taking shots at your enemy or building over them.

STORM BLOCKING

Another fun way to use building to overcome your opponent is with storm blocking. If you can lay down walls fast enough you can prevent your opponent from escaping the storm, or delay your opponents ability to escape the storm. The trick to making this technique work is to find a location that has some natural barriers already like hills or mountains, and to set yourself along the edge of the storm. As enemies come running in to escape the storm, throw down walls, ramps, and platforms to keep them out in the storm for as long as possible. Even if the storm doesn't kill them completely, you'll make a dent in their health for an easier kill in the end. Storm blocking is even easier when playing with a squad and it's a technique that should be used as often as possible when you have the resources and notice an opportunity to use it.

USING SCISSOR STAIRS

If you've ever watched a professional match of Fortnite, or went up against really accomplished players, you've likely witnessed the scissor stair technique at least once. This is an advanced technique that's defensive in nature, but an excellent tool for moving upward while staying out of danger in the heat of combat. The idea behind the technique is to stair up below and above your character at the same time. Essentially you are creating a ramp that's overhead, and a ramp that you walk up at the same time. This is a highly effective tool for scaling mountains and moving about when you aren't sure if there is an enemy up above you, or when there is a known enemy with the high ground advantage.

Creating scissor stairs is simple to do and a technique that every Fortnite player should master. To do it you move your cursor upward and downward dramatically while stairing up. If you do it with the right spacing you'll create two parallel sets of stairs and you'll be right in the middle of that

sandwich. This technique burns through twice the materials of standard scissor stairs, but it's essential for safe climbing.

If you rely on scissor stairs, make sure to turn and lay down some platforms as you build upward to make it more difficult to collapse your structure. Otherwise you'll be collapsed down to your death with ease.

CLIMBING DOWN WITH PLATFORMS

Cliffs are a serious danger in Fortnite, but there are going to be times when you're stuck on the edge of one with an enemy attacking. In these situations your best bet is to jump off the cliff. No, we're not telling you to commit suicide, you just need to understand how to make use of platforms to safely move down cliffs without taking damage.

Platforms are a powerful tool for dropping down cliffs rapidly and safely. To make use of them you simply keep platforms enabled and attach platforms to the side of the cliff just below your character as you fall down. Land on one platform

and jump off it and lay down another platform to land on once again. Lay platforms regularly so that you don't take any falling damage and you can very quickly move down a cliff without being trapped in one position. This is an important technique for you to master, and is something that you should practice in a match to get the hang of. Gather up plenty of materials and practice climbing down a cliff as rapidly as you possibly can. Few enemies will follow you down the cliff, and you can easily get away to safety when being pursued. Without understanding how to climb down properly you'll find yourself trapped and with fewer escape options when confronting an enemy or a group of enemies.

WATCH FOR MATERIAL CHANGES

While in heated combat with an enemy that's also building, you can tell a lot about the supply of your enemies materials by just watching the different material types being laid down. Since Fortnite automatically switches from one material to another as the materials run out, you can see when your enemy is running low on materials by watching for the change from wood to brick to metal. As the enemy goes through each of the three material types you'll know that they are about to run out of materials which gives you a huge advantage if you still have a good reserve of materials to work with.

While building watch to see what materials the other person is building out of and keep an eye out for rapid material changes. While this could be intentional by your opponent, it's most likely caused by a low material count, especially when going from wood to brick or metal. When that change occurs, keep building rapidly while keeping in mind that you might have the edge over your enemy in just a moment. Watch for more material changes and signs that your enemy can't build any longer, and when that occurs strike out at your enemy rapidly to take them out. ⭐

Enhancing Your Character
with Premium Items

FORTNITE IS A COMPLETELY FREE-TO-PLAY GAME ON A BUNCH OF DIFFERENT PLATFORMS, which is why so many people have picked it up over the last year or so, but that doesn't mean that there's nothing to spend real money on. Even though you could just keep playing through one match after another with all the standard items, by spending a bit of money you can customize your character in an infinite number of ways. The creators of Fortnite were very smart, because they made it possible to modify your character in so many different ways through premium items and enhancements. These modifications can change the way your character looks, add on different looking tools or outfits to those characters, or even change what sort of dance moves and gestures the character can do.

Premium items are a lot of fun and they add some real character to Fortnite, but most of the time they are going to cost you some money to obtain. Sure, there are some free character enhancements in Fortnite,

but most of the best stuff is premium content that will cost you some money. We're going to go over all the different types of customizations that you have available to you, and how you can make use of them to modify the way your character looks. After you learn about all the different customizations, you'll know whether you want to get some customizations of your own and what sort of enhancements that you want to make to your own character.

Skins

Skins are one of the most important customizations that you can get in Fortnite, because they change the way that your entire character looks. There are female and male skins in all sorts of shapes and sizes, and it's simple to make your character look different. Whether you want your character to look like a cowboy, a helicopter pilot, a bank robber, a spy, a superhero or something else entirely, there are tons of skins to choose from in Fortnite. The best part of all is that most of the skins being offered are limited time items. That means that players end up looking very different from one another.

Skins can be obtained from the item shop, from exclusive deals through Amazon or PlayStation or through the Battle Pass by raising your tier level by completing different challenges. No matter how you obtain your skins, they will give you additional options to choose from when you play Fortnite, so that you can get a custom look that will help you stand out and create a character that you can be really proud of.

If you decide to purchase skins, they are usually one of the most expensive items in the item shop. Skins generally sell for between 800 and 2,000 V-Bucks depending on their rarity and the look that they offer. Greens cost about 800 V-Bucks, while Blues cost 1,200 and oranges cost 2,000 V-Bucks. Choose the skins that you like the best and enjoy the custom look that they give you in the game. Many of

the most expensive skins will also show up in the game far less, so that's something to keep in mind while choosing the items that you want to go with as well.

Pickaxes

Pickaxes are another favorite item for players to customize in Fortnite. These are the tools that you use to harvest materials with, or to beat down enemies with if you don't have a gun. While they start off looking like pickaxes if you haven't customized them in any way, there are a bunch of additional custom pickaxes that you can get for the game as well.

Transform your pickaxe into a dinosaur skull, a hammer of death, a shovel, a shark, or something else entirely with one of the many different custom pickaxes. Pickaxes are available as free achievements by gaining enough tiers, they are available as premium Battle Pass achievements and they are for sale in the item shop regularly as well. There are some very cool pickaxes, and there's nothing like customizing the way that your character looks while interacting with the world to make the game more exciting. Next to the skins themselves, the pickaxes are our favorite customization type of the game. When purchasing a pickaxe from the item shop they tend to be purple or epic rarity and cost 1,500 V-Bucks.

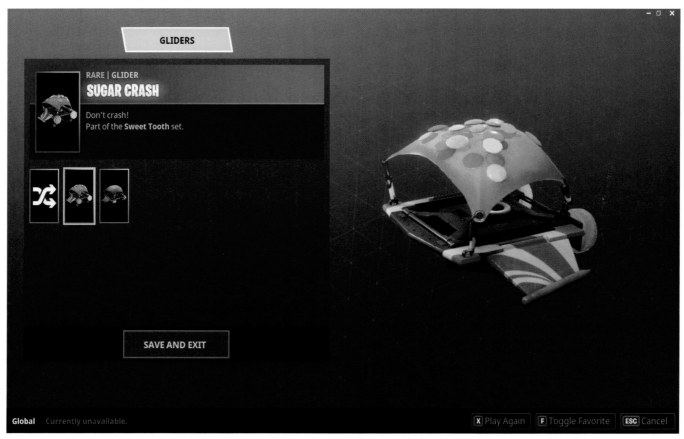

Gliders

As you leap out of the Battle Bus and fall down to your final destination your glider is out on full display. While the standard Fortnite glider doesn't look too bad, it doesn't have the same flash as a massive dragon kite, a sparkly bedazzled glider, a jet, a turtle shell, a spiky dinosaur back or one of the many other custom glider options released by the designers at Epic Games. There are so many different glider variations for you to pick up as a player on Fortnite that there is always something to be on the lookout for. It's true that gliders aren't used that often in the game, but custom gliders will still help you look as cool as possible as you make your way down to the ground.

Gliders can be obtained in a few different ways. Umbrellas can be obtained by winning matches, gliders can be obtained by purchasing the founders pack, completing Battle Pass challenges or by purchasing them out of the item shop.

EARNING UMBRELLAS

Each season a new umbrella glider is made available to players. This special glider is given out when you win a match in Fortnite. There is a different umbrella type for each season and they change each time you move from one season to the next. Using an umbrella glider is an excellent honor and usually a sign that you're a solid player. There is a paper umbrella, a paint umbrella, a snowflake umbrella and there will be other types issued in the future as new seasons come out.

BUYING OR EARNING ADDITIONAL GLIDERS

On top of umbrellas, there are all sorts of other glider types being given out to players in the game. Many can be unlocked by going through the Battle Pass challenges in the game. Just completing challenges and getting to high tier levels will unlock specialized gliders that you can use in future matches.

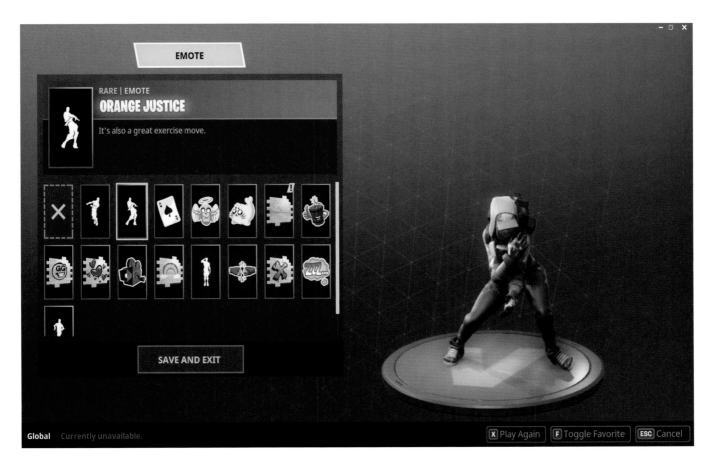

If you want something a bit more unique, or something that many players don't have, you can also purchase gliders in the item shop. There are dozens of different glider styles and they change on a daily basis, so check back in the shop often to see what is being offered currently. When you purchase Fortnite gliders from the item shop they range in price from 500 V-Bucks up to 2,000 depending on their rarity. The uncommon or green gliders cost just 500, while the legendary gliders come in at a stunning 2,000 V-Bucks each.

Emotes

Though emotes aren't visible unless you want them to be, they are one of the most enjoyable purchases that you can make in Fortnite. Emotes are gestures or dance moves that you can use to animate your character in the game. There's nothing quite like busting out into a goofy dance move after taking out an enemy, and with the different emote customizations you'll have a bunch of different moves to choose from.

These custom emotes include things like jumping up and down in celebration, waving, pretending to ride an imaginary horse, break dancing, tossing out money all over the place, breaking into some 1980s dance moves or spinning a basketball on your finger. There are so many different animations that you can probably find one for every single occasion. If you start to collect emotes, you can get them in a few different ways. The first and most direct way to gather emotes is to purchase them from the item shop, and there always plenty to choose from. These cost between 200 and 800 V-Bucks depending on what rarity they are. Uncommon or green costs 200, rare or blue costs 500 and epic or purple costs 800 V-Bucks.

If you aren't interested in purchasing individual emotes, you can unlock quite a few of them in the Battle Pass. There are usually 4 or 5 emotes each season, giving you quite a few to pick from if you can gain all the tiers from start to finish. It's also possible to obtain an emote as a Twitch Prime subscriber if you go through the steps to obtain your free Twitch Prime items.

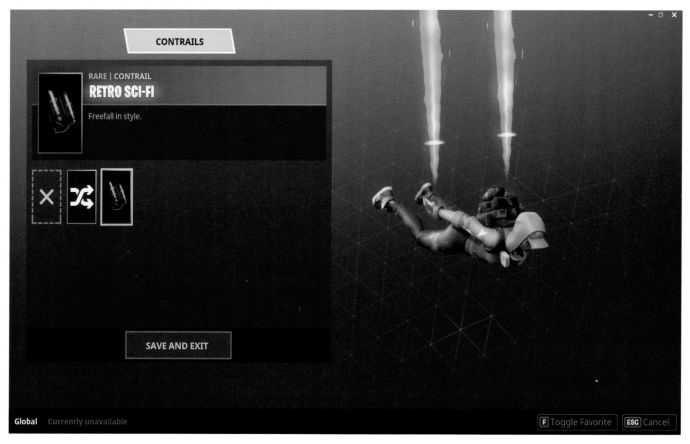

Contrails

There's another very cool customization in Fortnite known as contrails, and also known as skydiving trails. Without anything equipped in this slot your character will have air lines that come away from their arms and legs while falling down from the sky. These look pretty good themselves, but you can customize that look with all sorts of cool effects. Instead of sticking with the standard lines, it's possible to transform your character with bubbles, rainbow lines, stars, flames, sci-fi beams, spray paint, lightning and all sorts of other cool effects. These trails have only been available in the game since Season 3, and currently they can only be unlocked through the Battle Pass. Purchasing the Battle Pass will give you access to the trails for the current season, but won't give you access to any of the past season's trails. That means you should be able to obtain three or four trails throughout the season so that you can customize your character to look any way that you want while falling down through the air.

Emoticons

When actual emotes aren't diverse enough to show a feeling that you want to express in the game, or you just want to do something sillier, there are emoticons. These are essentially emojis designed to show up inside Fortnite, and there are tons of them. Emoticons don't really cost money, though you will obtain the majority of them if you spend the V-Bucks to purchase the Battle Pass each season.

Many emotes are available on the Fortnite Free Pass, which means that you can get them by just playing the game regularly. The rest all come from the Battle Pass and there are tons of them. There are 12 emoticons just from the Season 4 Battle Pass and there were many other opportunities to unlock these silly icons. Show off a rainbow, a chicken, a rabid dog, a banana, a laughing face, a flexing arm and many others as rewards for going up through the many different tiers of the Battle Passes.

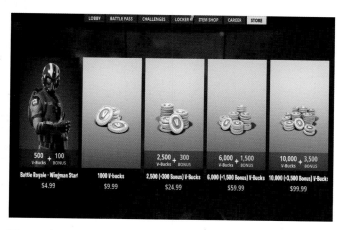

BACK BLING

Back bling or special backpacks are available to further customize your character in Fortnite. Most back bling items are available through the Battle Pass, through the Free Pass or as part of package deals that you purchase. Many item shop skins come with a back bling to match, and there are Starter Packs that you can purchase for Fortnite that come with a back bling item as well. There are all sorts of backpacks that you can get for your character, and they can be mixed and matched with other skins for a further element of customization as you play the game.

Sprays

Finally, the last bit of customization that you can use in Fortnite are the sprays. Whether you want to decorate your fort to make it beautiful in the game, you want to desecrate the wall of another player, or you just want to brighten up the game in some way, you can do all of that with the many different sprays. Sprays are available to players through the Battle Pass mostly and aren't available for purchase through the item shop at all. Players that are interested in getting their hands on sprays will pretty much need to purchase the Battle Pass. Sprays are occasionally given out as special events as well, for instance for visiting the E3 PR-Am event, or for participating in the Solo Showdown tournament.

The exclusive sprays are much harder to obtain, but will become part of your character's inventory for good as well.

Purchasing V-Bucks

Before going ahead with any of the Fortnite purchases such as items in the Item Shop, or buying the one of the Battle Pass packages, you'll need to obtain V-Bucks. The simplest and most straightforward way to do that is to purchase them. Fortnite V-Bucks range in price depending on the package that you purchase. At the low end a 1,000 V-Bucks purchase will cost about $9.99, while spending $59.99 will get you a whopping 7,500 V-Bucks. Prices will change depending on the market that you are in and the currency you use, but generally buying more V-Bucks at a time will save you money in Fortnite.

Once you purchase the V-Bucks through the marketplace that you use for your system, you can go ahead and use them for any purchases that you want on Fortnite. As long as you made the purchase with the right Epic Games account, you will be credited with your new V-Bucks the moment that you sign into Fortnite. Once you sign in you can go to the Item Shop and make a purchase. You can go into the Battle Pass and buy it or you can spend your V-Bucks on tiers for your existing Battle Pass. No matter how you want to use your V-Bucks, they are easy to obtain and to spend no matter what platform you play on.

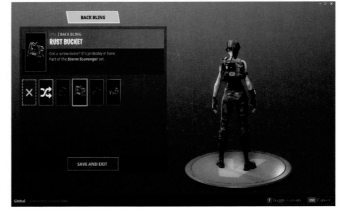

Free Character Enhancements

Most of the best customizations are offered to Battle Pass holders in Fortnite, or players that are willing to spend real money to purchase V-Bucks to spend in the Item Shop, but there are some freely available items to players that get on the game regularly. Even if you aren't going to spend real money on the game it's still fun to try and unlock all these items for your character.

UNLOCKING THE UMBRELLAS

One of the first things that you can do for each season is unlock your umbrella. By winning a single match of Fortnite you will qualify to get that season's umbrella which is always going to be unique. We know that winning a match isn't easy to do and that you'll have to work very hard to get the win, but if you manage to do so you will get a new umbrella glider to customize your character with. Do this at least once every single season and you'll have a bunch of umbrella gliders to show off as you play one game after the next.

EMOTICONS

There are tons of free emoticons you can get to really customize your character. These are available at all levels of the Free Pass and you can get some of these just by playing Fortnite regularly. Keep playing matches and you'll build up quite the collection without ever having to spend money on the Battle Pass.

BACK BLING

Back bling is like a back pack for your character that you can unlock by going through Free Pass challenges. There are several back bling items that you can get by leveling up, and they will give you yet another way to customize your character without having to spend money.

PICKAXE

By getting to some of the highest tiers that you can during each season of Fortnite, you can get a chance to unlock pickaxe tools for free. It will take daily play and completing most of your daily challenges in order to qualify for these special custom items, but you can get some pretty cool pickaxes over the seasons if you spend the time going through each of the different challenges diligently.

EMOTES

Free Pass players even have access to a few basic emotes. If you are willing to play enough of the game you can get some pretty basic gestures for your character as well, though you won't get any of the crazy dance moves that premium players are able to unlock.

With all the different customization options in Fortnite it can be pretty overwhelming deciding what you want when you are spending money on the items. Things are a bit different when you are getting them for free though. It's best to just go ahead and get as many of the different objects as you can, so you can create as many different looks as possible. They are free after all.

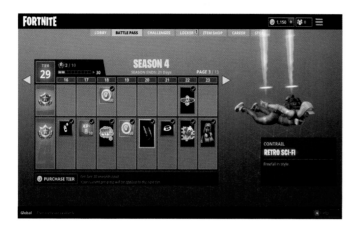

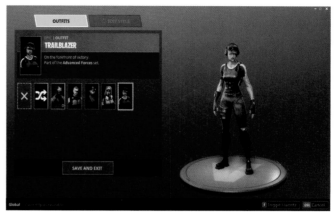

Battle Pass Enhancements

If you're interested in unlocking new content for Fortnite, the Battle Pass is one of the best ways that you can spend your money on the game. Instead of spending the cash to unlock a single skin, or to get yourself a new shiny glider, you could unlock a pass that will give you access to dozens of items. All these items can be unlocked just by playing the game like you always do, and you'll end up with a whole bunch of achievements for your efforts as well. The Battle Pass currently costs just 950 V-Bucks and will give you a bunch of different rewards just for purchasing it initially. After you have the pass you will have a bunch of other items to try and work your way toward as well, as long as you are patient enough and willing to work hard, you should be able to get all sorts of cool customizations for your character.

Each season's Battle Pass comes with a different theme, and many of the items will fit that theme flawlessly. There will always be some unique items included in the pass too though, and it's up to you to unlock anything that you like in the pass.

The Battle Pass has a total of 100 tiers, that will give you over 1,000 V-Bucks, skins, gliders, contrails, emotes, tons of emoticons, banners, load screens and even more for you to try and unlock. All of those different items can be yours as long as you complete the necessary challenges to unlock

them, and you don't really have to be that good at the game in order to get the items, you just need to play frequently.

UNLOCKING THE MANY DIFFERENT PASS ITEMS

In order to unlock as many of the Battle Pass items as you can, there are two tasks for you to complete. You must finish off as many of the different challenges as you can, including the daily and weekly challenges, and you must level up your character as much as you possibly can. Leveling your character will reward you with Battle Stars along the way, and so will completing the many different challenges. Gain enough levels and complete enough challenges and you will reach tier 100 of your Battle Pass. Do that and you've unlocked nearly all the Battle Pass content and will have a bunch of new customizations to play around with in the game.

Unlocking Twitch Prime Exclusive Items

While it generally costs money for customizations in Fortnite, there are a few different ways that you can get stuff for free as well. One of those ways is by having an Amazon Prime account that you've connected to Twitch. This gives you a Twitch Prime account that you can use to get some exclusive items for Fortnite.

GET A TWITCH ACCOUNT

If you don't have a Twitch Account already, consider getting one. Twitch is a platform that people stream video game content and other types of content on. It's a place that you can go to watch top pros play Fortnite and other leading online games. If you are interested in watching some quality gameplay, Twitch is an excellent place to be a member of. Even if you don't want to watch quality gameplay, it's worth joining Twitch just so you can qualify for the free items for Fortnite if you already have Amazon Prime.

GET AN AMAZON PRIME ACCOUNT

Amazon Prime is an excellent service for people that like to purchase things off of Amazon that will help them get items shipped straight to home in just two days without paying for shipping. This service also comes with a bunch of additional perks, like a streaming video service and Twitch Prime. If you already have an Amazon Prime account you just need to know what your Amazon account information is to get Twitch Prime. If you don't yet have Amazon Prime, it is worth considering if you buy items online frequently, or you want to gain access to all the other perks that the service offers. A membership costs about $120 per year currently, and it can be paid monthly or annually depending on your preference.

LINK YOUR PRIME ACCOUNT

If you already have Amazon Prime, you can go ahead and link your Amazon account to your Twitch account to make it a Twitch Prime account. Doing that will give you the ability to subscribe to one streamer's channel each month for free, and also to unlock an exclusive Fortnite package of items.

To link your Amazon Prime account to your Twitch Account, sign into Twitch, and visit the connections tab. While in this tab select Twitch Prime. From there you will be asked to sign into your Amazon account and you will have successfully transformed your Twitch account into a Twitch Prime account.

LINK YOUR EPIC GAMES ACCOUNT

Now that you have Twitch Prime, you can easily unlock your exclusive Fortnite content. To do that you just need to give Epic Games permission to access your account, sign into your Epic Games account and you will be credited with the loot. This is simple to do as long as you know your Epic Games information, and you will be immediately credited with the pack that is being given out. Different free packs are given out to Twitch Prime members over time, so you can get multiple packs, and you will get different sets of items depending on which season the game is on.

WHAT COMES IN A PACK

The Twitch Prime packs are different each time, but generally you get a skin, an emote, a pickaxe, and a back bling when you link your Twitch Prime account to your Epic Games account. The pack will be credited to your account the next time that you sign into Fortnite and you'll have a present waiting for you. Congratulations! You just unlocked an exclusive pack of items!

Unlocking PlayStation Plus Exclusive Items

These packs generally include a skin and a back bling, but each pack is a bit different so it's important to check and see what's being offered currently. If you aren't sure about where to find this unique skin pack, just visit store. PlayStation.com and enter Fortnite into the search box. From there select "See All" and you should be able to find an item tagged with Exclusive that also says PlayStation Plus in the name. This will be your bonus pack and you can add it to your account from here.

If you are signed into your PlayStation Account when accessing the store, you will be credited with your exclusive items right then and there. If you aren't, you'll need to sign on to get the items in the proper account.

Making the Most of Premium Items in Fortnite

Don't worry about getting every trendy item in the game, unless that's something that you want to do, and instead focus on the items that you really like the most. Just one unique skin and set of additional items can make your character look different and help you show off your personality in the game.

Choose the look that suits your own personality the best, and you'll enjoy your character in Fortnite even more. There are plenty of people that spend far more than they need to on customizations without taking the time to get good at the game. Don't make this mistake. Instead take advantage of all the low-cost customizations that you can, grab any and all free customizations, and only purchase the ones that mean the most to you. Spend the rest of your time enjoying playing the game. ★

FEATURED ITEMS

PICK YOUR STYLE!

COLLECT THE SET!

2 of 2

CUDDLE TEAM LEADER

Outfit

 2,000

TAT AXE

Harvesting Tool

 800

Note: These items are cosmetic

1,150 +   0

20:45:02

SQUAT KICK

Emote

800

GOOGLY

Glider

800

COMMANDO

Outfit

800

RILLIANT STRIKER

Outfit

1,200

TIDY

Emote

500

LUCKY

Harvesting Tool

500

rant no competitive advantage.

All About the Battle Pass

IF YOU'RE A SERIOUS FORTNITE PLAYER, THE BATTLE PASS MIGHT BE THE BEST WAY TO SPEND MONEY ON THE GAME. IT ADDS VALUE TO YOUR FORNITE GAMING HOURS IN A NUMBER OF WAYS. This addon costs about 950 V-Bucks currently, but it's an investment that can enhance your experience with the game and give you more to look forward to each time you log on to play. If you want to get more out of your Fortnite gaming time and effort, investing in the Battle Pass is key.

The Battle Pass isn't something you should purchase your first time playing Fortnite, but if you find yourself spending an increasing amount of time on the game, it's definitely worth a look. This premium enhancement offers unique value to heavy players and is almost an essential upgrade for serious Fortnite fans.

What Is Battle Pass?

The Fortnite Battle Pass is a premium addon that you can put onto your Fortnite account for one season of the game. During that season your character will gain access to premium challenges and a whole bunch of other unlockable items that you can't get as a free pass character. By purchasing the Battle Pass you are placed into the premium bracket, where you will earn experience faster, you'll unlock a bunch of additional items and you'll have a chance to get a bunch of premium items that you would otherwise have to purchase individually through the item store.

To obtain the Battle Pass you need to purchase a minimum of 1,000 V-Bucks and then go to the store to purchase the pass right within Fortnite. Do that and you'll immediately gain access to the additional content awarded by the pass. From the moment that you start with the new pass you'll get some introductory items and perks, and over time as you tier up by completing challenges you'll unlock additional perks. It's one of the most cost-effective purchases you can make in Fortnite, and it's an excellent way to improve your experience.

Is Battle Pass Worth it?

The Battle Pass costs roughly 950 V-Bucks currently, which is worth around $9.50 if you purchase the small pack from Epic Games, which makes it a somewhat expensive enhancement to make to your game of Fortnite. With that said, you get a lot for your money and if you are a good enough player, you might not have to buy another Battle Pass next season either!

LOTS OF FREE ITEMS

The number one reason that players want the Battle Pass in Fortnite is for all the premium items that the passes can unlock if you play regularly enough. There are a bunch of special items incorporated into the Battle Pass that can be triggered over time. Players don't need to win matches consistently to unlock these tier items, they just need to complete their challenges and log on the game regularly and they can unlock pickaxes, back bling, skins, spray, loading screens, banners, emoticons, skydiving trails, gliders, emotes and other special prizes from the pass. These prizes are all spread out throughout the tier levels of the Battle Pass and you can see what is available before ever purchasing the Battle Pass to begin with. If you aren't sure about whether or not the Battle Pass is worth the money, take some time to look through all the items that you'll get and then decide if you want it or not.

FREE V-BUCKS

A major perk of having the Battle Pass is access to V-Bucks as you go up through the tiers. As you complete challenges and move up toward Tier 100 of the pass you'll actually unlock hundreds of free V-Bucks. Players on the free pass in Fortnite also have a chance to unlock some free V-Bucks and could theoretically purchase the Battle Pass with those after going though enough seasons, but Battle Pass owners unlock many more free V-Bucks and have the opportunity to purchase many more premium items with their winnings over time.

ENHANCED EXPERIENCE FOR YOU AND FRIENDS

Gaining levels in Fortnite each season will make you feel like a more accomplished player and will also give you another goal to shoot for while helping you tier up your Battle Pass. The Battle Pass itself comes with a built-in feature to help you level up your character more effectively, and that's experience boosts. There are personal XP boost bonuses, friend XP boost bonuses and also bulk XP rewards for

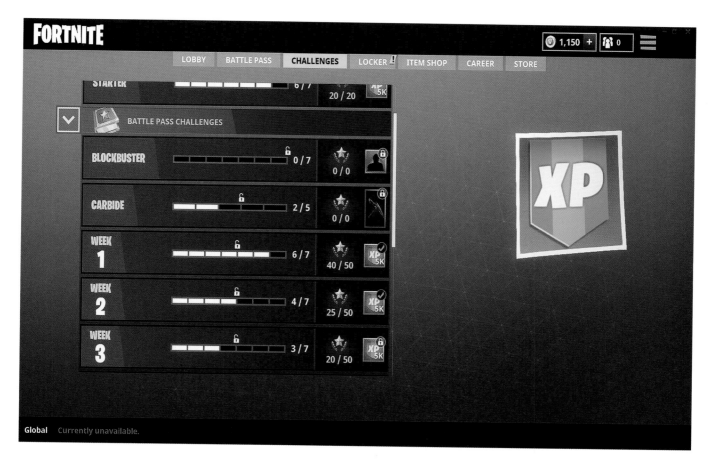

getting different tiers in the Battle Pass. These bonuses will help you level up your character in Fortnite more quickly, so that you can hit level 100 faster and enjoy all the added Battle Stars that you get while working your way up.

MORE CHALLENGES

As the owner of a Battle Pass for the current season, you gain access to weekly challenges that free players don't have. All these additional challenges give you new ways to unlock stars to raise your tier level up higher and higher. If you are diligent about completing most of the challenges that appear each week, you will tier up to higher Battle Pass levels and unlock a bunch of different rewards that you couldn't get with the standard game pass.

The trick to making the most of your Battle Pass is to keep an eye on the many different challenges that are released and to try and keep up with them as you go. It's okay if you get a week or two behind on your challenges, you can complete multiple weeks' worth of challenges at the same time as you play through matches of Fortnite. Just make sure you are getting those matches in, and that you are working on improving your skills and notching kills in the game.

Leveling up Your Battle Pass

After you purchase the Battle Pass it's up to you to level it up so that you can get access to all those excellent rewards and bonuses. What that means is that you need to get on regularly and complete all the different challenges connected to your Battle Pass. This isn't really difficult to do, but it is time-consuming, especially for newer players that will have trouble completing some of the elimination challenges. Don't let this discourage you if you are taking awhile to gain tiers towards your Battle Pass, just keep working at it and you will speed up with time as you get more comfortable with everything.

COMPLETE DAILY CHALLENGES WHENEVER POSSIBLE

The very first step to increasing your Battle Pass is to finish all the daily challenges that you can. Try to log on at least once a day whenever you can to tackle daily challenges that pop up. These challenges change each and every day, and give you additional chances to earn Battle Stars that will tier you up through your Battle Pass. Do your best to complete each challenge the day that it is issued. For many players the challenges will take between 30 minutes to one hour to complete, but some challenges are more difficult than others.

COMPLETE WEEKLY CHALLENGES

As a Battle Pass holder you will have access to exclusive weekly challenges that you can complete on top of the daily challenges. These challenges are available each and every week of the current season, and they will remain available for the life of the season until you complete them.

What that means is that if you pick up the Battle Pass on the fourth week of the season, you can go back through and complete the first four weeks' worth of challenges in one day if you like. Each weekly set of challenges come with special rewards and a special theme, and when you complete them all you'll receive a bunch of Battle Stars.

New weekly challenges aren't accessible until the following week if you complete all your current challenges, but it will take some time to get through all the challenges, even if you play on a daily basis. Players that want to get to the highest tiers of the Battle Pass should make it a goal to complete every one of the weekly challenges. Doing so might even grant them a special reward!

LEVEL YOUR CHARACTER

The last way to tier up your Battle Pass is to level your character. Gaining levels in Fortnite awards you with Battle Stars that will raise your tier level as well. Each time you gain a level that ends in everything but 5 or 0 you will receive a single Battle Star. When you level up to a level ending in 5 or 0, you will receive 5 Battle Stars or 10 Battle Stars respectively. Getting enough character levels will help you gain a bunch of Battle Pass tiers as well, making it even easier for you to reach the maximum tier level.

Unlocking Battle Pass for Life

Many players that purchase the Battle Pass in Fortnite treat the purchase as one that they need to keep making at the beginning of each season. This isn't necessarily true. Sure, the Battle Pass is a powerful addon that really improves the game and makes it worth playing, but that doesn't mean that you need to spend money each season in order to benefit from all that it offers. If you don't mind hoarding all your V-Bucks that you get from leveling up through the tiers, you shouldn't have too much trouble buying your next Battle Pass without spending any real money, and you can actually go from one season to the next with a Battle Pass that you never spent real money on.

GENERATING THE NECESSARY V-BUCKS

As you move through the tier levels in Fortnite, you'll pick up additional V-Bucks for free that you can use to save for your next Battle Pass. These V-Bucks aren't difficult to come by and you'll get them naturally just for moving up through your Battle Pass and unlocking the items and boosts that you want anyway. In order to get enough V-Bucks to buy a whole new Battle Pass, you normally need to get up into the mid 60s for your Battle Pass tiers. Do that and you'll have the money to purchase the next pass and you can continue to enjoy the benefits that it offers you.

SAVING THE V-BUCKS

Once you've gone through the steps to earn at least 950 V-Bucks with your current Battle Pass, you just need to save those bucks for the next season of Fortnite so you are ready to purchase your pass and get grinding up the tiers all over again. Make sure that you always have at least 950 V-Bucks stored away in your account, and you should have no trouble getting your next pass.

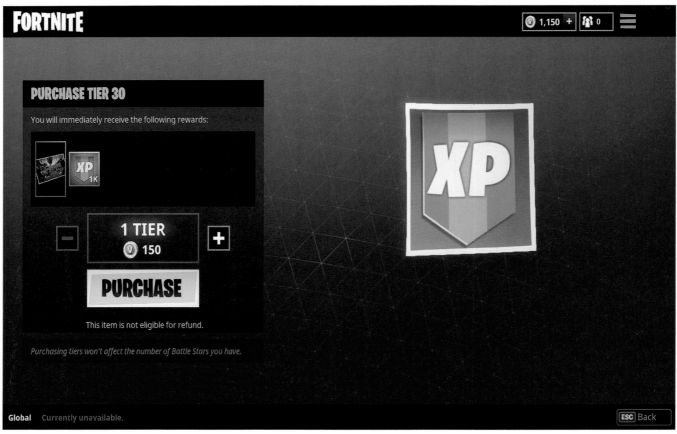

SPENDING YOUR EXTRA V-BUCKS

If you are a player that's gone through the top tiers of the Battle Pass, you might have some extra V-Bucks past the 950 that you need to purchase your next Battle Pass. You can feel free to spend these extra V-Bucks on any items that you want to enhance your character, or to save them toward more expensive items in the future, just make sure if you spend them that you hold onto the V-Bucks that you need to purchase your next pass.

As long as you are careful, and you go up through all the tier levels in Fortnite, you should have no trouble purchasing the Battle Pass each and every season without paying for it. It's easy to do, gets you started earning the best premium items in the game, and will give you something to work toward each season as you improve your game.

Making the Most of Battle Pass Challenges

The most beneficial part of having the Battle Pass is all the challenges that come along with it each and every week. These challenges are released throughout the season, so you need to continually check for new updates every single week. As you try and tier up your Battle Pass, you should be completing as many challenges as you possibly can in order to do so. If you're getting on and completing those challenges you'll be making the most of your Battle Pass and unlocking all the tiers that you need to unlock the free V-Bucks and special items and boosts all tied to the pass itself.

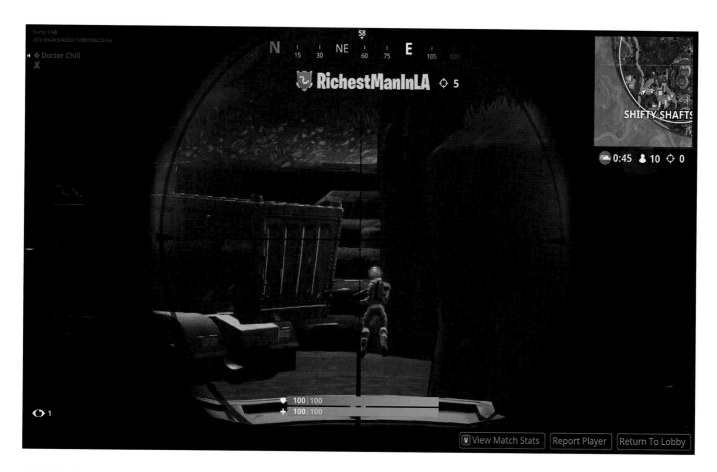

CHECKING CHALLENGES REGULARLY

Challenges get updated daily and weekly when you're a Battle Pass owner. That means that in order to take advantage of all the different challenges that come out you really need to be checking them regularly. Each time you get onto Fortnite, take a minute to read through the latest challenges and learn how to make use of them as efficiently as possible. Read through your challenges and consider writing them down before starting your matches. Once you know the challenges you can start working towards completing them. This will take some time, but as long as you keep the different challenges in mind as you go through matches you shouldn't have too much trouble finishing off each and every one of them.

SPEED RUNNING CHESTS

Every week there is going to be at least one chest-based challenge. You will be asked to loot seven chests from a specific location. This is a pretty straightforward task and shouldn't be too difficult. The best way to accomplish this

goal reliably is to learn a few chest locations for the area, and drop down to them as fast as possible at the start of the game. If you are dropping quick enough you should be able to get your hands on at least one chest each time that you go to a location. From there you can play the standard game and work on getting some of your other challenges, or if you are eliminated you can start a new match and go for another chest in the same location once again.

STACKING CHALLENGES

If you get behind on your challenges, or you just have weekly and daily challenges that line up, you can actually stack up the same challenges and complete two or three at the same time. This is a powerful strategy that will help you get through more challenges fast and will lead to moving up through the tiers more reliably. The challenges that stack the best are normally gun-specific elimination challenges. It's possible to get two or even three challenges that all tell you to eliminate players with a pistol. That means that each

pistol elimination you get is checking off tasks on multiple challenges. Focus on stacked challenges whenever you have them, because they are the most effective way to unlock those Battle Stars and to increase your tiers. You'll notice that it's very easy to do this if you fall behind on your weekly challenges. You can easily burn down a bunch of challenges at the same time without realizing that you are doing it when you are behind on your weekly challenges, and that will make it easier for casual gamers to gain tiers on Fortnite.

ELIMINATIONS WITH UNPOPULAR GUNS AND ITEMS

Whenever you need to complete an elimination challenge with a weapon that you don't personally like using, there is a simple strategy that you can use to accomplish this. Join up on your own without Fill in Squads or Duos. Then knock enemies down with guns that you do enjoy using. Once they are down, use the weapon that you don't really like to finish them off. That's all you need to do to get those eliminations and they should be pretty straightforward.

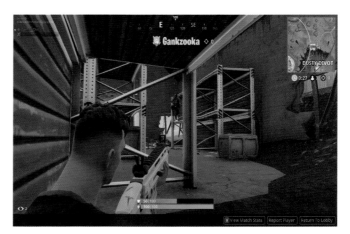

Just make sure that you are carrying around one of the weapons that you need to get eliminations with, and you should be scoring those kills before you know it. This also works when you get a challenge for trap eliminations or for when you need to do damage to enemies with your pickaxe. You can beat them down with your pickaxe after you've already downed them. You can also lay a trap down right next to their downed body and wait for it to go off as they crawl around.

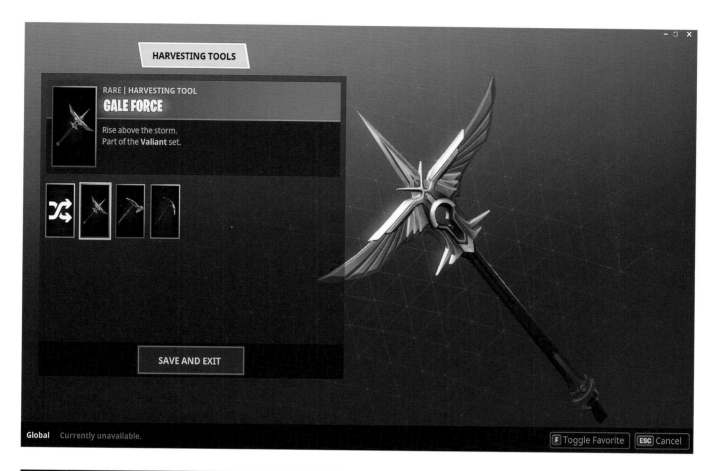

ENJOY THE BATTLE PASS

The Fortnite Battle Pass is one of the best investments that you can make if you play Fortnite frequently. It's good for a few months of premium play, and it will even pay for itself if you choose to spend all the V-Bucks you earn throughout the season on your next pass. Just make sure that you are completing your challenges, that you are getting on regularly and that you are playing your best in every match. You'll come to love the Battle Pass and will have trouble playing Fortnite without it once you get used to having it.

Follow all the details in this guide and you should have no trouble gaining tiers and free items from the Battle Pass. It's another tool to make your time in Fortnite more enjoyable, but will only work well for you if you are making full use of it. Take the time to try some of the challenges, play regularly and you'll be getting a bunch of the loot from the Battle Pass, even if you don't complete every single tier. ⭐

Fortnite Pros

PLAYING FORTNITE IS A GREAT WAY TO HAVE CASUAL FUN, BUT THERE ARE OTHERS THAT TAKE THE GAME TO A WHOLE NEW LEVEL. Players like Ninja and TSM_Myth don't just focus on winning matches, but like any true professional, they focus on being the best in the world at their craft, all the time. They can be described as Fortnite pros. But what makes a pro? What does it take to be a pro? And how can you best learn from the pros' video streams, to help you improve your own game in the meanwhile?

All of these topics and more are covered in-depth in this section of the book. If you've already mastered the gameplay fundamentals of Fortnite in the earlier chapters and you're interested in becoming pro, or just want to learn who to follow and how to use their pro tips and insights to help you be better at the game, here is some more info on these folks and how they can help you.

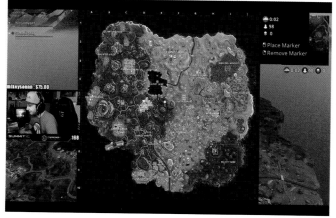

Who Are the Pros?

There are literally millions of Fortnite players currently, but only a handful of them can be the very best. The following pages feature a combination of highly skilled players and well-known experts. These guys are all excellent at the game, and they all have streams or videos for you to watch. If you're interested in learning more about the game, or seeing what pro-level Fortnite play looks like, take a look at footage put together by one of these top players.

They aren't listed off in any particular order, and each of these top-level players has something special to watch. If you're trying to get better at the game, or just looking for high level Fortnite play, it's worth witnessing a few of these players in action.

Cizzorz

Cizzorz is an entertaining YouTuber that also happens to be an excellent Fortnite player. He's taken part in many professional Fortnite tournaments and consistently wins matches in solos, duos and squads. He can be found on Twitch or YouTube and is known for winning Fortnite matches stylishly.

HighDistortion

HighDistortion is well-known for his unique voice and his excellent gameplay commentary. This player began his online career as a professional Gears of War player and is now one of the very top Fortnite legends. He has a really deep voice and a relaxed commentary style while going through slightly slower-paced matches. He's definitely worth following for elite play, and is a favorite to watch online.

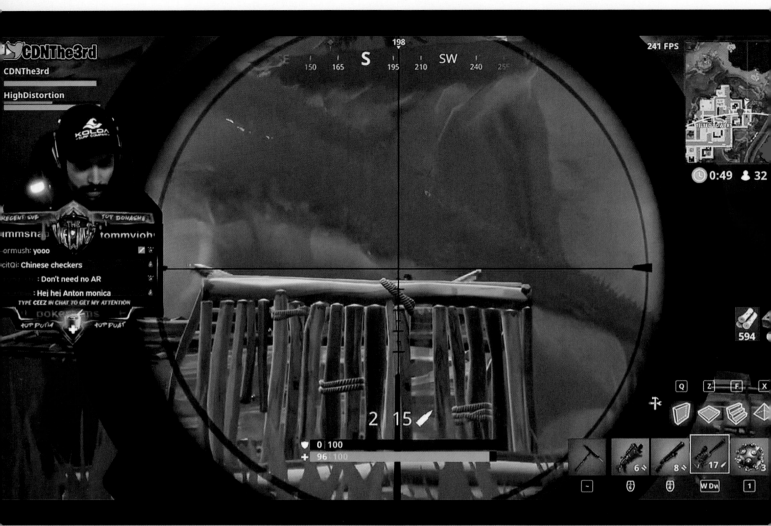

CDNthe3rd

CDN is a leading professional Fortnite player with a huge YouTube and Twitch following. He plays regularly with HighDistortion and can regularly be found streaming on Twitch. This streamer is known for his comedic style and is pretty entertaining to watch while also teaching quite a bit about the game as well.

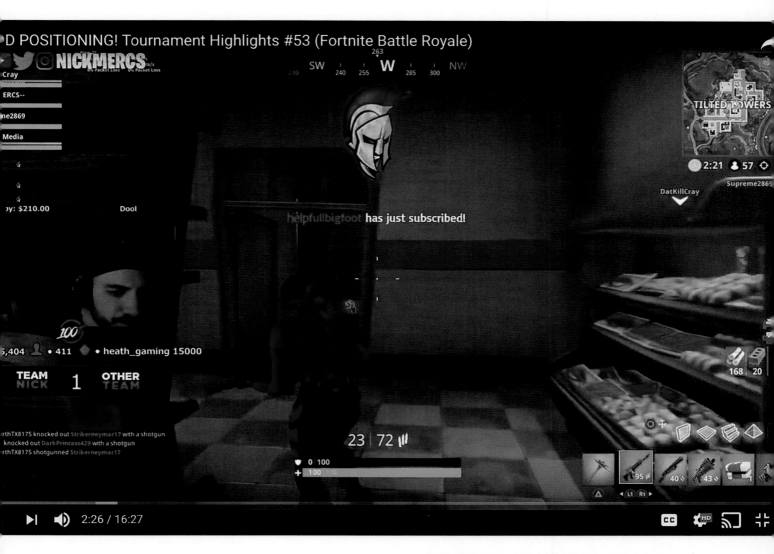

NickMercs

While not as famous as some other Fortnite pros, NickMercs started off as a professional Gears of War player and is known for his excellent aim. He's not the strongest builder, but his sharpshooting makes up for that and he's able to take the top spot in a huge number of regular matches and tournaments for that very reason. He's well-known for getting insane kill counts during combat and often records more than 20 kills in a match.

Daequan

Daequan is one of the most laid-back YouTubers on this list with an excellent following on YouTube and Twitch. He can also be found paired up with TSM_Myth regularly, one of the best builders in all of Fortnite. This makes for some very entertaining gameplay footage and it's always a learning experience when watching these pros in action.

TSM_Camills

Camills is a Twitch and YouTube user and is less well known than many of the other pros on this list. He's an excellent player though and pairs up with the likes of Myth and Daequan in matches. He's known for having a good mix of building skills and weapon accuracy and frequently takes wins in Fortnite. Camills doesn't offer too much commentary during matches, but is still entertaining to watch for high level gameplay.

Avxry

Avxry is a very popular YouTube streamer that puts videos and streams up daily showing off top level Fortnite gameplay. This player has a more chilled out personality than most. He was born in 1997 and is well-known for having high numbers of Fortnite kills. He's collaborated with Ninja in the past and that really helped to drive up his popularity while showcasing just how good he is at the game.

TSM_Myth

TSM_Myth, also known as ImTheMyth, is one of the best and most well-known Fortnite players today. He's recognized as one of the leading combat builders in the game and is a member of the professional team TSM. This top player is huge on YouTube and Twitch and maintains a channel with hundreds of millions of video views. If you're trying to figure out how to improve your building, watch some Myth videos and you'll pick up a bunch of tips and tricks.

Ninja

Ninja is the most well-known of all the Fortnite players at the professional level, and he's also one of the most entertaining to watch. He's twitchy, he's funny and he always offers some sort of learning experience during his matches. Ninja has an interesting play style that mixes excellent aim with building skills, and that's why he wins so many of the professional level tournaments. With hundreds of thousands of Twitch subscribers

it's clear that he's the frontrunner in Fortnite in terms of popularity, but he's also one of the most skilled players on this list.

Any one of these professional level players could teach most new or even experienced Fortnite players how to get better. The trick is figuring out how to learn from their gameplay and incorporate it into your own matches. If you are trying to figure out how to improve your play in Fortnite, you can really enhance your strategies by watching the pros play.

Learning from the Pros Using Twitch and YouTube

Pros aren't just exciting to watch play Fortnite, they're also educational. Some pros take the time to explain the decisions that they make throughout a match, and others just add in fun commentary about the game. Either way, there is a lot that you can learn by watching professional Fortnite players as long as you are looking for information. Whether you are trying to figure out the best way to get above your enemy, or you just want to know a good starting location in your drop location of choice, you can learn all these things and much more from professional players.

WATCH STREAMS AND VIDEOS REGULARLY

The most obvious way that you can improve with help from professional Fortnite players is to watch them play regularly. If you are tuning into their streams on a daily basis you are going to pick up a bunch of information about how to play the game effectively. This knowledge will help you become more aware of what you should be doing during matches and what skills you have to work on. Of course, just watching professionals play in Fortnite isn't going to make you a pro player, but will give you the information that you need to improve rapidly, and also help you take out more technically skilled players that can't match your strategies.

WATCH FOR BUILDING TECHNIQUES

In Fortnite, shooting works pretty much the same no matter what skill level you are at, and building is where the real pros are proven most of the time. The majority of the best players can build circles around lower skilled players. When you watch professional matches, pay attention to how the players build and look for new techniques that you aren't that familiar with. If a player is ramping up or climbing in a way that you haven't tried before, make note of the technique and give it a try in your next match. Keep a list of the different ideas that you've picked up from matches, or even save video clips of these techniques so that you can implement them in your own matches. You'll improve as a builder by learning these new techniques and practicing them, and may soon find yourself topping the leaderboards as well.

PAY ATTENTION TO DROP LOCATIONS

One of the easiest things you can learn from professional Fortnite players is useful drop locations. These players have run through thousands of matches and they know which locations are most effective for them after all that time. By just trying out their drop locations you can very quickly establish useful locations for yourself.

If you aren't that good at starting out in Fortnite, take the time to watch a few pros play through a dozen or more rounds, and make a list of all the starting locations that they use, along with details like which part of the building they drop on or in, and how they move on from that starting location. With this information handy, test out all the different starting locations to see which ones you like the best. Keep toying with the new locations until

you find something that you are very comfortable with and that is helping you get started with good gear without dying immediately. Once you find a proven location that is working well for you, start dropping there as often as possible so you can get more familiar with it and improve your skill in that starting spot.

LISTEN TO COMMENTARY

Not all professional players provide any sort of commentary during their videos at all, but many of the best players offer information about the decisions they are making, or insights into the game itself. If you want to learn something from the pros, just listen to what they have to say during combat. They might utter just a few sentences now and then, but that little bit of information could be what gives you what you need to start beating your enemies.

WATCH THE SAME PROS REGULARLY

Some pros like TSM_Myth are more well-known for building than anything else. Others like NickMercs are known for their shooting skill and lack of need for complex building techniques. If there's one specific aspect of your game that you want to improve, it's improtant to find a pro that's very good at that skill and to watch them regularly. Keep a close eye on Myth over time if you want to learn how to build. Watch the way that NickMercs uses his superior shooting mechanics to take out opponents without building much more than basic structures. No matter what sort of player you want to be in Fortnite, you can learn how to do it more effectively with a little bit of insight from other pros. Take the time to watch their gameplay and you'll get more familiar with how to emulate it yourself.

Becoming a Fortnite Pro

Watching professionals play the game is a lot of fun, and it's exciting to hear that pros like Ninja can make hundreds of thousands of dollars playing Fortnite. But you don't just have to sit back and watch others have success with the game! Following the pros may make you want to dream the dream and go pro as well, and it's not impossible. If you are dedicated enough to the game and have a catchy angle or good sense of humor, maybe you can become a Fortnite pro over time, or even find success posting YouTube videos or streaming on Twitch.

Becoming a pro isn't easy, and it's certainly not guaranteed to anyone, but with persistence, practice and the right approach, anyone has a chance to reach the highest levels of Fortnite.

Keep reading to learn what you need to do to become a professional Fortnite player. The advice is simple, the follow-through is not—that's what separates the pros from the amateurs in most sports.

WATCH THE PROS

The first step to ascending to pro status is to spend a lot of time watching the current pros play the game. You'll pick up techniques and strategies that would take you a great deal of time to acquire yourself. By watching professionals, you'll gather a lot of tips, tricks and shortcuts to help you improve as fast as possible. Once you start applying this knowledge in your own gameplay, you'll find yourself suddenly getting better, faster, than many of your friends.

LEARN THE BASICS

By consuming resources like this guide, and watching videos, you can learn all the basics of Fortnite to at least be decent at the game. Take the time to fully understand basic building techniques and how to make the best use of each weapon in different situations. After you have a good understanding of the game mechanics and how they work, you can move on to developing your skills through repetition and become an advanced player.

MASTER YOUR TECHNIQUE

Whether you're a racecar driver, a doctor, or a musician, there is no substitute for muscle memory—when your reflexes act quicker than you can think because you have spent so much time training. Once you understand the basics of Fortnite, and you've watched plenty of professional player videos or streams, it's time to practice, practice, practice! Start working on your building techniques in a less populated location like Wailing Woods. Get proficient at building common structures as fast as you possibly can and try to climb up and down in the air as quickly as possible. After you can fluidly build through the air and get to any location you want using structures without thinking about it, you can turn your attention to improving your combat skills.

Once you are a competent builder, you can move on to improving your reaction timing and fighting skill. To do this you need to drop in hostile locations with lots of enemies. Drop in places like Tilted Towers, Pleasant Park and Loot Lake, where you will see plenty of combat. Work on using your building skills and your increased shooting ability to take out as many players as you can. Keep repeating this technique until you are notching multiple kills before you get taken out. Once you reach this point, you will have a decent enough technique to build on towards becoming a top player.

PRACTICE REGULARLY

With the fundamentals mastered, and as you develop the skills the top-notch players employ, you are ready to put these two things together and become better at the game. Drop down in well-tested starting locations and practice getting the best positioning that you can. Try to make smart decisions as you move around the map, but also don't run away from too many fights. By learning how to handle enemies and all kinds of situations, you'll become more confident, more effective and more successful in Fortnite.

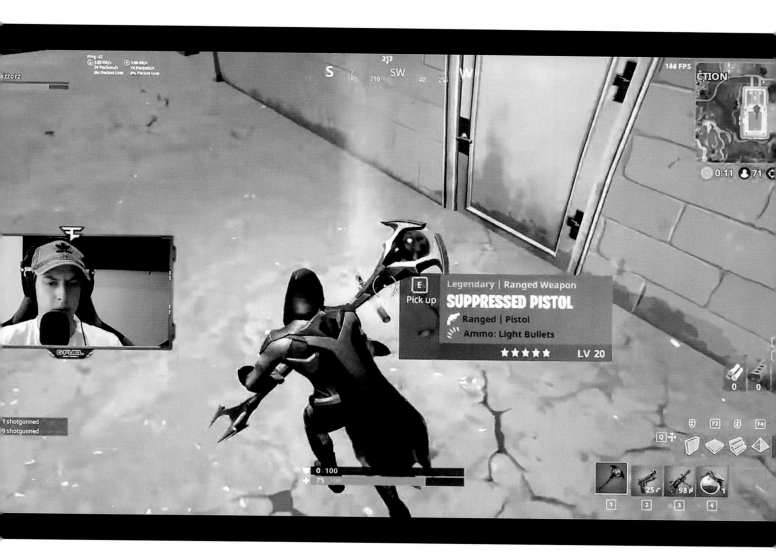

Professional Fortnite Matches

Fortnite is exploding in popularity and Epic Games is focused on making Fortnite one of the best competitive E-Sports available today. For both of those reasons it's a great time to dive deeper into Fortnite. Even if you have no interest in participating in E-Sports, you can enjoy watching the high-level matches played in all sorts of different professional tournaments.

Epic Games has set aside money for hosting professional tournaments, and with the record growth of the game it's only a matter of time before there are professional Fortnite tournaments around the world. Serious players that want to become pros should start practicing as soon as possible, because the opportunities are multiplying.

Whether you dream about being a professional Fortnite player, or you just want to improve your own gameplay while watching some entertaining matches, it will boost your game if you become more familiar with the top pros and start following them. Fortnite already has plenty of professional level players that can teach you something big or small. Keep working at your own skills in the game, watch those high-level matches and eventually you might find yourself teaming up with, or against, some of those famous Fortniters! ★

Conclusion

FORTNITE IS STILL A VERY YOUNG FRANCHISE THAT'S GOING TO KEEP GROWING FOR A LONG TIME. This guide provides a solid starting point to improve your game, and answers the questions most of the folks have when they want to get better. But while playing Fortnite has become a national phenomenon, many gamers can't make it through the initial learning curve without getting frustrated.

By poring through this guide carefully, you'll start to learn ways that you can get more out of Fortnite. You'll learn which items make the most sense to pick up. You'll learn how to create cool sniper towers and how to get the best of enemies that have more training than you. It's an exhilarating feeling when you come up against a foe that wants to win just as much as you, and you overcome them.

While this guide won't make you a pro, only you can do that, it can definitely help you get more out your gaming time. Even if you're not a top tier player, this guide will surely prevent you from getting stuck at the bottom of every match.

Read, soak up more info where you can, adapt your strategy, practice, and learn to love Fortnite while improving your game! That's what this guide is all about—any player can have more fun if they get even a little better at the game, or learn how to pick up some sweet animations and accessories to personalize and customize their Fortnite experience. Now, it's your turn!

You can learn everything you need to know to get started on the right path. After reading through every section, you'll have a good understanding of the key concepts behind Fortnite, and be ready to practice and improve on your own. Before heading into a match thinking that you're

going to take everyone out because you read the chapter on building and the chapter on weapon use, realize that you need to spend lots of hours practicing the advice in those chapters to make it work for you.

With the knowledge that you gain from this book, you should be able to beat other players who have a level of experience equal to yours, and maybe even some who are a little better than you! Just make sure you are getting in those practice reps. We can help coach you up on how to improve your game, but only you can put in the hundreds or thousands of hours of practice it requires to be great! ★

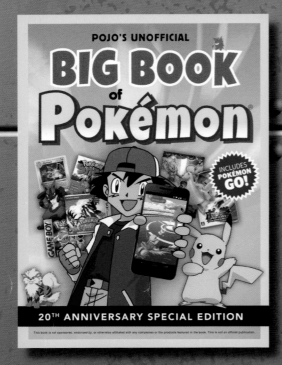

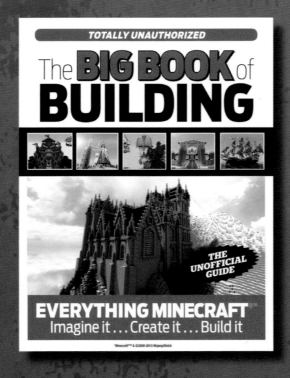